ALL CHANGE!

Best practice for educational transitions

Our titles are also available in a range of electronic formats. To order, or for details of our bulk discounts, please go to our website www.criticalpublishing.com or contact our distributor, NBN International, 10 Thornbury Road, Plymouth PL6 7PP, telephone 01752 202301 or email orders@nbninternational.com.

CRITICAL
PUBLISHING

ALL
CHANGE!

Best practice for educational
transitions

**Rhiannon Packer with Catherine Jones,
Amanda Thomas and Philippa Watkins**

First published in 2021 by Critical Publishing Ltd

British Library Cataloguing in Publication Data
A CIP record for this book is available from the British Library

ISBN: 978-1-913063-57-3

This book is also available in the following e-book formats:

MOBI ISBN: 978-1-913063-58-0
EPUB ISBN: 978-1-13063-59-7
Adobe e-book ISBN: 978-1-913063-60-3

Portrait illustration by Élisabeth Eudes-Pascal represented by GCI

Cover and text design by Out of House Limited
Project management by Newgen Publishing UK
Printed and bound in Great Britain by 4edge, Essex

Critical Publishing
3 Connaught Road
St Albans
AL3 5RX

www.criticalpublishing.com

Paper from responsible sources

CONTENTS

MEET THE AUTHORS

RHIANNON PACKER

I am based at Cardiff Metropolitan University, having previously worked at the University of South Wales (USW) for nearly 14 years. The transition from one higher education (HE) institution to another was huge, despite the many similarities. I trained as a secondary school teacher and worked for a year and a half before leaving to undertake research for a PhD. I then returned to school for another seven years ... I then entered HE. I am the lead author for this book.

CATHERINE JONES

I am education cognate group research lead and academic manager for innovation and technology in the faculty of life sciences and education. I have over 20 years' experience in HE and have also worked in other education sectors. I have carried out collaborative research and teaching in the following areas: developing professional practice; safeguarding; technology enhanced learning; and mentoring and coaching. I have been involved with managing transitions across different sectors of education.

AMANDA THOMAS

I am currently a senior lecturer in early years education at USW, delivering on a range of education modules. In 1997, I began teaching in a primary school and successfully led the early years provision. I have also taught in further education for four years, training childcare practitioners. I teach on a range of modules at USW which include transition.

PHILIPPA WATKINS

I am currently a senior lecturer in early years
education at USW. I originally trained as a
secondary school English teacher and worked
in a number of different schools in South Wales.
I was head of English for four years. I worked in
Istanbul teaching English as a foreign language
for a year and worked for Basic Skills Cymru
for two years as a project leader. I have been
lecturing at USW for ten years, teaching on a
range of education modules and acting as a
year tutor.

ACKNOWLEDGEMENTS

The authors would like to acknowledge and thank all the participants and settings who gave their time to take part in the research for this book. Without you, there would be no book.

Thank you to Julia Morris from Critical Publishing for her help, guidance and support throughout the writing process, making it straightforward and manageable.

Diolch yn fawr i bawb am eu cyfraniad hael i'r llyfr hwn.

Finally, thank you to our families who supported us throughout by creating space and time for us to work on this book. Diolch o galon i chi gyd.

I. INTRODUCTION

Rationale

This book is inspired by the ongoing discourse and policy debates surrounding transitions in education. There is a clear recognition that learner experiences of transition, particularly the early ones, can have a long-term impact on educational achievement as well as general life experiences and well-being (Field, 2010). A life-course theory approach (in conjunction with other theories) has been used to examine successful transitions. Life-course theory provides a useful theoretical framework as it recognises that all stages of an individual's life are intertwined with each other, with the lives of those around them (overlapping with Bronfenbrenner's (1979) ecological systems theory) and with the experiences of those who have gone before (World Health Organization, 2018). This book, therefore, adopts the stage-like approach of life-course theory (supported by other behaviourist theory) to help gain a more complete picture of transitions. In doing so, it considers the prior experiences, ongoing ones and reflections of all those involved: the learner, the parent and the practitioner.

Issues around definitions

The importance of providing effective transitions in education continues to be a key feature of policy, practice and research (Ingram et al, 2009; Colley, 2007). It has been recognised for some time that transitions can be problematic and require support, particularly for those children and young people who might be vulnerable, struggling with social and emotional issues or *at risk* (Ecclestone, 2007). There is also significant research which associates transitions between different stages of education with a dip in achievement (Galton and McLellan, 2018). It is important, therefore, to be clear on what exactly is meant by the term *transitions*, and to which phases in education it can be applied. This is especially important as there still remains an inconsistency in the way the term *transition* is used and understood.

Traditional approaches to transitions in education considered it as a *one-point* event, focusing on, for example, the first day at a new school or in a new class. However, transitions are now understood to involve more than this, and while they do involve some sense of *movement* or *transfer*, they are not just that. As the learner progresses through the education system there are other significant changes. These can include issues of identity as well as developmental and emotional changes that last as long as the individual needs to make such a change (Welsh Government, 2017). Considering transitions in this context acknowledges that the term *transition* is as much about the psychological routes needed in adapting to the change event or disruption (Kralik et al, 2006) as it is to do with the change itself.

At its most straight forward, transition can be seen as a natural process (Davis et al, 2015), a movement from one institutional setting or activity to another (Lombardi, 1992). Galton and McLellan (2018), in their study of research on transitions, conceived it metaphorically as a bridge, aiding the movement of a student over time from A to B. This approach is evident in early-childhood-development theory, especially in terms of Piaget's arguments for *'ages and stages'* (Carey et al, 2015) a concept criticised as being too linear and reflecting *'Western or Eurocentric epistemology'* (Downes et al, 2018, p 443). As settings become more inclusive, so transitions need to take into account more vulnerable children for whom transition may pose a greater risk than for others (Symonds, 2015; Davis et al, 2015). For example, Davis et al (2015) point out that a key issue faced by learners with special educational needs is that they are expected to adhere to pre-established systems and processes. However, it is arguable that it is not only vulnerable pupils that experience this risk. If transition is regarded only as a surface phenomenon, a matter of transference from one place to another, then more fundamental and complex meanings and issues may be missed. Downes et al (2018) raise the issues of disguised meanings, citing Bourdieu's (1986) concept of symbolic violence, as a part of the transition process that might be ignored. This refers to the idea of subconscious subordination, where the place travelled to is the place of power and so for all those pupils experiencing transitions there is an expectation that they must conform to the place to which they will move.

Issues surrounding transition

While transitions are considered by many as a normal part of the journey through formal schooling (Topping, 2011), there is evidence to suggest that early transitions often set the stage for future positive or negative ones (Rosenkoetter et al, 1994). For some children the transition from one class or setting to another compromises academic progress (Ashton, 2008) and sometimes well-being (Marks, 2004). This is of significance to policy makers because the experience and learning of children and young people in education impacts on society and economy (Ecclestone, 2007); both of which now present significant challenges. The European Commission (2018) makes it clear that managing transitions in educational settings should be seen as an opportunity to provide learners with key life skills, as well as promoting equity and excellence. This is because change has become an increasing pattern within the workforce, caused by things like demographic change, changing employment patterns and technological advancement (Ecclestone, 2007).

In the United Kingdom, key transitions are given significant emphasis. These include pivotal ones between stages in learning, for example the transition from Key Stage 2 to Key Stage 3, which has long been an area of focus of policy in both England and Wales (Hodgkin et al, 2013). However, there are other more subtle transitions to do with subject choices, different teachers and different classes that also need to be considered. Research suggests that transitions are often associated with underachievement, a 'dip' in pupil attainment (Sutherland et al, 2010) and negative impacts on well-being.

To be effective, therefore, transitions need to be seen as more than a shift in place, limited to a specific time and part of an academic process. Instead, it needs to be acknowledged that transitions are in fact *'fundamental features of social life* and *one of the defining characteristics of everyday life of "becoming"'* (Field, 2010, p xvii). This means that the concept of transition should embrace a much broader notion of education than simply the learning experienced within formal institutions at a given time. It includes a tacit learning about identity and self, what a person can become and where that person is located socially and spatially.

Ways to approach transitions

The approach taken in this book, therefore, is to consider transitions in terms of cultural *'rites of passage'*. According to Martin-McDonald and Biernoff (2002, p 347) these *'rites of passage'* can be quite varied and often occur when there is a change in *'cultural expectations, social roles, and status'* in terms of changes to position, in relationships or situational changes. What they share, however, is a sense of movement through key aspects of life. Van Gennep's (2019) theory of rites of passage identifies three distinct phases to these transitions.

1. Rites of separation where the individual is removed from what is already known.
2. Rites of transition as the individual is in the transition, a kind of *no-man's land*.
3. Rites of incorporation, where the individual is absorbed into a new environment.

This idea of three phases is also found in Bridges and Bridges (2019), who identify the three parts in terms of a beginning, a *'fallow'* time and an ending. What these models propose is the idea of transition having a linear trajectory composed of starting and finishing points. However, the simplicity of this often overlooks that transition is often ongoing and quite complex and does not always follow a chronological trajectory.

As well as the concept of *'rites of passage'*, there is also the approach taken by Lam and Pollard (2006) to consider. They argued that there are two types of transition taking place that need to be differentiated:

1. the horizontal transitions (from change of one context for another); and
2. the vertical transitions (when the child becomes established in the new setting).

The first type is the shift between place and the second is the adaptation to the new place. These, involve shifts in identity and agency (Ecclestone, 2007) and can be a time of *'intense accelerated development demands that are socially regulated'* (Lam and Pollard, 2006, p 125). Therefore, it is important that all involved are given a voice. Ranson's (2000) *'pedagogy of voice'*, which requires active listening and learning from the opinions and feelings of others, goes some way to help understand perspectives (Wertsch, 1991), and find ways to improve participation and teaching and learning (Wei, 2017).

Structure of this book

The transitions discussed in this book are about both the change from one setting to another and the shift from one identity to another. Its focus is predominantly on those in compulsory education; however, an international perspective is also considered. The voices heard are not just those of the learners, but also those who provide or facilitate a support system around them – the parent and the practitioner – and they speak of the process of change as experienced by all of them.

CHAPTER 2: THEORIES OF TRANSITION

Chapter 2 provides a number of key theoretical frameworks through which transitions are explored in this book. It presents the key theories and explains how they are used to explore transitions from the learner's, the parents' and the practitioner's perspective. The chapter enables the development of an analytical lens through which experiences of transitions discussed later in the book can be analysed. It highlights the fundamental importance of reflection, the use of theory to support practice and the necessity of preparing all stakeholders early for transitions.

CHAPTER 3: VULNERABLE TRANSITIONS

Chapter 3 considers transitions from the perspective of learners identified under the Equality Act (UK Government, 2010) as being vulnerable. This includes learners who are refugees, asylum seekers, traveller children, children with identity and gender questions and children with disabilities. It looks at the evidence that shows these children, some of whom are not considered to have special educational needs (SEN), additional learning needs (ALN) in Wales or additional support needs (ASN) in Scotland (DfE, 2018; NASEN, 2014), still require additional support particularly when making the change from one educational setting to another.

CHAPTER 4: LESSONS IN LISTENING 1: THE LEARNER'S VOICE

Chapter 4 explores how learners interpret, navigate and make sense of their experiences during various transition points and across various transition boundaries. Learner responses to different transitions are analysed and explored from both a theoretical and practical perspective. Of particular interest are the changes in the agency and identities of children as they settle into different educational settings. The chapter argues that there is a need to listen to learners about their transition experiences and to use this to inform future practice.

CHAPTER 5: LESSONS IN LISTENING 2: GIVING VOICE TO THE LEARNER'S SUPPORT SYSTEM

Chapter 5 recognises the value of the parents' or caregivers' voice during transitions experienced by their children. It considers how past experiences of transition by the parents themselves can influence how their children approach the transition. It argues that the role of the parent or caregiver needs to be given importance as they are often the most significant influence on the learner's successful transition and are key in preparing the learner for forthcoming change. It argues that while schools do involve parents, it is often a one-way relationship with schools leading the agenda, more so as the learner progresses through the education system.

CHAPTER 6: PRACTITIONER DISCOURSE: PREPARING AND SUPPORTING TRANSITIONS

Chapter 6 explores practitioner perceptions of transition. It examines the role that they play in instigating and facilitating that process and analyses how procedures around transition are timed and controlled. It explores the fundamental purposes of the transition process and recognises the importance of the practitioner's role in its effectiveness. It argues that practitioners must be fully aware of the significance of transition activities upon individuals and should consistently reflect on clarity of expectations of not just the pupils, but the parents/caregivers and themselves as well.

CHAPTER 7: INTERNATIONAL PERSPECTIVES ON TRANSITIONS

Chapter 7 considers transitions from an international perspective with a particular focus on European countries. It explores some of the commonalities and differences of transitions experienced elsewhere and identifies some themes to explore. By looking at what is done elsewhere, observations can inform further discussions in the United Kingdom. It explores the theoretical context for these observations, as well as providing more specific experiences of those who have lived through it.

At the end of each chapter, readers will find reflective questions that encourage further deep thinking about what has been discussed, as well as suggested reading if further information is required.

Keys

The settings from which data was collected are identified below.

- Further-education (FE) college 1
- FE college 2
- FE college 3
- Secondary school 1
- Secondary school 2
- Sixth form
- Year 1
- Year 2
- Reception 1
- Reception 2
- Key Stage 2 (KS2)
- Special school 1

The key used to identify the voices is as follows.

- Parent: Pt
- Learner: L
- Practitioner: P
- Head of Year: HoY
- Head of Key Stage 4: HKS4
- Special Educational Needs Co-ordinator: SENCo
- Secondary teacher
- SEN teacher 1
- Transition officer

ALNCo, SENDCo and SENCo are terms used to describe the role of practitioners who co-ordinate special needs provision in educational settings. We have opted to use the latter form SENCo as this term still has currency across the United Kingdom.

References

Ashton, R (2008) Improving the Transfer to Secondary School: How Every Child's Voice Can Matter. *Support for Learning*, 23(4): 176–82. [online] Available at: https://doi.org/10.1111/j.1467-9604.2008.00391.x (accessed 7 June 2020).

Bourdieu, P (1986) The Forms of Capital. In Richardson, J (ed) *Handbook of Theory and Research in the Sociology of Education*. Westport, CT: Greenwood Press.

Bridges, W and Bridges, S (2019) *Transitions: Making Sense of Life's Changes*. Boston: Da Capo Lifelong Books.

Bronfenbrenner, U (1979) *The Ecology of Human Development: Experiments by Nature and Design*. Boston, MA: Harvard University Press.

Carey, S, Zaitchik, D and Bascandziev, I (2015) Theories of Development: In Dialog with Jean Piaget. *Developmental Review*, 38: 36–54. [online] Available at: https://doi-org.ezproxy.cardiffmet.ac.uk/10.1016/j.dr.2015.07.003 (accessed 7 June 2020).

Colley, H (2007) Understanding Time in Learning Transitions Through the Life Course. *International Studies in Sociology of Education*, 17(4): 427–43. [online] Available at: https://doi.org/10.1080/09620210701667103 (accessed 7 June 2020).

Davis, J M, Ravenscroft, J and Bizas, N (2015) Transition, Inclusion and Partnership: Child-, Parent- and Professional-led Approaches in a European Research Project. *Child Care in Practice*, 21(1): 33–49. [online] Available at: https://doi.org/10.1080/13575279.2014.976543 (accessed 7 June 2020).

Department for Education (2018) *Keeping Children Safe in Education*. London: HMSO.

Downes, P, Nairz-Wirth, E and Anderson, J (2018) Reconceptualising System Transitions in Education for Marginalised and Vulnerable Groups. *European Journal of Education Research, Development and Policy*, 53(4): 441–46. [online] Available at: https://doi.org/10.1111/ejed.12311 (accessed 7 June 2020).

Ecclestone, K (2007) Lost and Found in Transition: The Implications of 'Identity', 'Agency' and 'Structure' for Educational Goals and Practices. Keynote Presentation. In *Researching Transitions in Lifelong Learning*. [online] Available at: https://semanticscholar.org/paper/Lost-and-found-in-transition-%3A-the-implications-of-Ecclestone/31db123c152d22f4c6ec4130f378a73f00fa73a5 (accessed 12 March 2020).

European Commission (2018) *Continuity and Transitions in Learner Development*. [online] Available at: https://schooleducationgateway.eu/downloads/Governance/2018-wgs3-learner-development_en.pdf (accessed 22 April 2020).

Field, J (2010) Preface. In Ecclestone, K, Biesta, G and Hughes, M (eds) *Transitions and Learning through the Life Course*. London: Routledge.

Galton, M and McLellan, R (2018) A Transition Odyssey: Pupils' Experiences of Transfer to Secondary School Across Five Decades. *Research Papers in Education*, 33: 255–77. [online] Available at: https://doi.org/10.1080/02671522.2017.1302496 (accessed 7 June 2020).

Hodgkin, K, Fleming, S, Beauchamp, G and Bryant, A (2013) Perception to Reality: Pupils' Expectations and Experiences of the Primary–Secondary School Transition. *Educational Futures*, 6(1): 28–140.

Ingram, R, Field, J and Gallacher, J (2009) Learning Transitions: Research, Policy, Practice. In Field, J, Gallacher, J and Ingram, R (eds) *Researching Transitions in Lifelong Learning*. London and New York: Routledge.

Kralik, D, Visentin, K and Van Loon, A (2006) Transition: A Literature Review. *Journal of Advanced Nursing*, 55(3): 320–9. [online] Available at: https://doi.org/10.1111/j.1365-2648.2006.03899.x (accessed 7 June 2020).

Lam, M and Pollard, A (2006) A Conceptual Framework for Understanding Children as Agents in the Transition from Home to Kindergarten. *Early Years*, 26(2): 123–41. [online] Available at: https://doi.org/10.1080/09575140600759906 (accessed 7 June 2020).

Lombardi, J (1992) Beyond Transition: Ensuring Continuity in Early Childhood Services. [online] Available at: https://files.eric.ed.gov/fulltext/ED345867.pdf (accessed 12 March 2020).

Marks, N (2004) *The Power and Potential of Well-Being Indicators: Measuring Young People's Well-Being in Nottingham*. London: New Economics Foundation.

Martin-McDonald, K and Biernoff, D (2002) Initiation Into Dialysis-dependent Life: An Examination of Rites of Passage. *Nephrology Nursing Journal*, 29(4): 347–53.

NASEN (2014) Transition: A Quick Guide to Supporting the Needs of Pupils and Their Families When Moving Between Educational Settings. [online] Available at: https://nasen.org.uk/uploads/assets/d120f943-7f8b-48c6-bc5b0d2ab448c54d/transition.pdf (accessed 7 June 2020).

Ranson, S (2000) Recognizing the Pedagogy of Voice in a Learning Community. *Educational Management and Administration*, 28(3): 263–79.

Rosenkoetter, S, Hains, A and Fowler, S (1994) *Bridging Early Services for Children with Special Needs and Their Families: A Practical Guide for Transition Planning*. Baltimore: Brookes.

Sutherland, R, Yee, W C, MacNess, E and Harris, R (2010) *Supporting Learning in the Transition From Primary to Secondary Schools*. Bristol: University of Bristol. [online] Available at: https://bristol.ac.uk/media-library/sites/cmpo/documents/transition.pdf (accessed 12 March 2020).

Symonds, J (2015) *Understanding School Transition: What Happens to Children and How to Help Them*. London: Routledge.

Topping, K (2011) Primary–Secondary Transition: Differences Between Teachers' and Children's Perceptions. *Improving Schools*, 14(3): 268–85. [online] Available at: https://doi.org/10.1177/1365480211419587 (accessed 7 June 2020).

UK Government (2010) *Equality Act*. London: HMSO.

van Gennep, A (2019) *The Rites of Passage* (second edition). Chicago: University of Chicago Press.

Wei, X (2017) Using Student Voice in Learner-centered Course Design. *Educational Research and Reviews*, 12(7): 403–14.

Welsh Government (2017) Flying Start - Annex: Transition Guidance. [online] Available at: https://gov.wales/sites/default/files/publications/2019-07/flying-start-transition-guidance-for-professionals.pdf (accessed 18 February 2020).

Wertsch, J (1991) *Voices of the Mind: A Sociocultural Approach to Mediated Action*. Cambridge, MA: Harvard University Press.

World Health Organization (2018) *The Life-Course Approach: From Theory to Practice. Case Stories From Two Small Countries in Europe*. [online] Available at: http://euro.who.int/__data/assets/pdf_file/0004/374359/life-course-iceland-malta-eng.pdf (accessed 2 March 2020).

INTRODUCTION

2. THEORIES OF TRANSITION

Rationale

This chapter explores key theoretical frameworks that help construct a deeper understanding of transition, its function and impact. Key theories are initially presented in Table 2.1 and then examined from three perspectives:

1. the learner who experiences the transition;
2. the key stakeholders, such as parents or caregivers, who support the learner;
3. and practitioners who facilitate the transition process.

Exploring the theory of transition provides an opportunity to gain a deeper understanding of it as a concept and it helps to develop an analytical lens through which transition can be analysed. This, combined with meaningful reflection, can help extend current knowledge and understanding which can then be applied to practice (Gouthro, 2019). This means that the transition does not happen in isolation and thus enables practitioners (and stakeholders such as parents or caregivers) to view the transition process in a more seamless way. It also encourages the early preparation of learners for the transition, which enables them to settle into the new environment more easily.

How key theoretical frameworks relate to practice

The following theoretical frameworks have been identified as useful in exploring and developing an understanding of transition from the perspective of the learner, stakeholder and practitioner. While other theories may support aspects of transition, the five frameworks identified in the grid help give a comprehensive understanding for the development of a tailored approach.

The theories presented in Table 2.1 are demonstrated below with examples from the learner, different stakeholders and practitioner perspectives.

Table 2.1 Theories that support understanding of transition

THEORETICAL FRAMEWORK	KEY POINTS	IMPLICATIONS FOR PRACTICE
Ecological systems theory (Bronfenbrenner, 1979)	Identifies five key systems of relationships and structures that surround the individual and influence development. 1. Microsystem: the individual's relationship with others, interpersonal interactions and immediate surroundings. 2. Mesosystem: interactions of elements of the microsystem with each other, eg between family and practitioners. 3. Exosystem: elements of the microsystem which do not affect the individual directly but could indirectly, eg parent's workplace. 4. Macrosystem: the cultural and societal beliefs that influence an individual's development. 5. Chronosystem: the interaction of the four identified systems with each other, how they affect and change each other over time.	Recognition that the child does not exist in isolation and is constantly influenced by environment, relationships and culture. Practitioners and stakeholders need to understand the child in the context of multiple environments – including the one they are entering.

THEORETICAL FRAMEWORK	KEY POINTS	IMPLICATIONS FOR PRACTICE
Sociocultural theory of cognitive development (Vygotsky, 1978)	Social interaction with more skilled individuals (the more knowledgeable other (MKO)) plays a fundamental role in the development of cognition. A *'zone of proximal development'* (ZPD) exists whereby the individual is able to learn with support from the MKO. Every function in the child's cultural development appears twice - first between people (interpsychological) and then inside the child (intrapsychological).	Practitioner provides the ZPD through scaffolding and enabling the support of the MKO. Learners can support each other. Effective communication to ensure stakeholder involvement and awareness of key transition points is essential in order to ensure that they can support learners effectively and be supported themselves.
Life-course theory – developed in the 1960s (Hutchison, 2011)	Interdisciplinary theory studying life trajectories across multiple stages in life. Recognises that developmental processes extend beyond childhood. Duration (the time between transitions) is as important as the transition itself. Focuses on cultural and historical contexts. An authentic appreciation of human agency.	Practitioners should consider the learner's voice in supporting effective transition and take into account the diverse context of some learners. Transition can be supported in many different ways and one approach might not suit all learners. Practitioners should plan and prepare learners for transition in plenty of time before the change occurs. This includes effective communication between a range of stakeholders.
Communities of Practice Theory (Lave and Wenger, 1991; Wenger, 1998)	A group of people with a shared area of interest who work together for collective learning.	Practitioners recognise what can be learnt through relationships and communication (both informal and formal) with all stakeholders involved in the transition process.

THEORETICAL FRAMEWORK	KEY POINTS	IMPLICATIONS FOR PRACTICE
'Les Rites De Passage' (van Gennep, 2019)	*'Rites of Passage'* occur during a life course when an individual moves from one group to another or makes a transition from one status to another.	The theory provides practitioners with ideas about the experiences during rites of passage which involve rituals of separation, disorientation and assimilation. As such, understanding this theory can facilitate useful strategies for supporting transitions.

The learner

In terms of understanding the concept of transition, research generally focuses on the perceptions of staff working with children and young people. However, in line with life-course theory, listening to the learner's voice is important because of the complexities of the transitional experience. This is an area of research that has rapidly gained momentum (MacDonald, 2009; Di Santo and Berman, 2012). According to the Organisation for Economic Co-operation and Development (OECD, 2017) the participation of children in planning transition activities gives them ownership and provides stakeholders with a better understanding of the challenges they face and the support they need. This is the case in Finland, Norway and Sweden where the voices of children are listened to with regards to how they feel about transition, acting as co-researchers as they contribute to the production of knowledge (OECD, 2017). This evidences agency, a key feature of life-course theory, by providing opportunities and space for the learner to understand and act upon their world (Waller, 2009). Understanding agency enables the learner to create change by expressing their desires and negotiating and interacting with their environment. The concept of community of practice (Lave and Wenger, 1991) is also important as learners come together to define their identity in a school environment.

To gain a sound and thorough understanding of transition, practitioners should consider children's perspectives (MacDonald, 2009). It is important to listen to the learner (Jindal-Snape and Miller, 2008), an understanding underpinned by life-course theory and the United Nations Convention on the Rights of the Child (UNCRC) (UNICEF UK, 1989). Children and young people are the ones who experience the change first-hand and have valuable knowledge to offer (Galton and McLellan, 2018). This is explored by Perry and Dockett (2011), whose research focuses on the child's perspective and views them as experts in their own lives. Their research illustrates how children's perceptions of what is needed are different from practitioners'. An example given by MacDonald (2009) identifies the difference in perception of catching the bus to school between practitioners and pupils. Practitioners thought it might be a source of concern for the pupils, yet pupils saw it as an exciting part of the day. Another example given from a setting was to do with support for children experiencing transition. Each pupil was assigned an older 'buddy'; however, discussions with the younger pupils found that they thought sharing three to four buddies per class was preferable to having one each. When the buddies – considered as the *'more knowledgeable other'* (Vygotsky, 1978) – were consulted, they felt that younger children needed more visits to school in order to help them cope with the transition (Di Santo and Berman, 2012). In all cases pupil voice needs to be considered in conjunction with what it is feasible for practitioners to do.

HOPES AND WORRIES

Loizou's (2011) research with six-year-olds found that children starting school for the first time faced both *empowering* aspects – such as bigger space, new experience and social encounters – and *limiting* aspects such as lack of fun and a rigid structure. While friendships, peer relationships and knowing the rules of school were important to children and young people on starting school (Di Santo and Berman, 2012; O'Toole et al, 2014) they also worried about having less play in school and associated school with homework and academic skills – a particular concern for pupils moving into secondary (O'Toole et al, 2014). Hugo et al (2018) also found young children starting school were concerned about negative relationships (*'I don't want to get picked on because my brother Tyler got picked on'*) and positive relationships (*'some big kids will play with me and I will be on their team'*). They also worried about organisational skills.

Lockers in particular seemed to cause difficulty, with one child vividly describing the chaos between lessons as all students tried to get to their lockers and access books for the next lesson.

(O'Toole et al, 2014, p 124)

O'Toole et al (2014) found striking similarities between primary and secondary school learners when they talked about their worries and hopes. They both experienced mixed feelings of nervousness and excitement when moving to another setting (O'Toole et al, 2014). The physical practicality of getting to school was of great importance for children in McDonald's (2009) study when they recalled their experiences of transition. This is something that is not usually mentioned in other studies. Children also discussed negative feelings and did not like being separated from their parents on starting primary school. This point highlights the significance of the microsystem (Bronfenbrenner, 1979) and how important it is for adults to remember that when learners transition the context of their mesosystem significantly changes (O'Toole et al, 2014).

WHY IT IS IMPORTANT TO BE PREPARED

Listening to the learner's voice makes it clear transition is more than just a physical event. Ackesjö (2013, p 387) argues that *'children enter the transitions process long before they actually (physically) enter or visit school'*. Her research shows that helping children think about their previous educational setting identity can be important during the transition process. This raises two important points: first, that staff/adults need to focus on where a learner has come from in order to help them navigate and understand their new environment. Secondly, that staff/adults need to have some understanding of the previous learning environment or context in order to help the learner cope with the change. This is because, as Markström (2005, cited in Ackesjö, 2013) suggests, for some children moving from one setting to another is not like crossing a bridge but rather crossing a ditch which can be very challenging to navigate.

In terms of preparing secondary school learners for university, James et al (2010, cited in McPhail, 2015) report that only half of first-year university students felt that their final year of school prepared them appropriately. They also suggest that better partnerships are needed between schools and universities. Positive and well-established partnerships are important because *'the prospective student faces the challenge of leaving established relationships, forming new relationships and embarking on advanced study'* (Bradley, 2012, p 101). Bradley (2012) states that transitioning to university is usually discussed within the sociology of education and suggests that a social–psychological framework such as life-course theory is helpful in understanding the process. Life-course theory encourages a rich understanding of individual life trajectories by considering the policy, social context, and patterns of family and friendship influence within which life decisions are made (Bradley, 2012, p 101). Listening to the learner voice continues to be important because young people should be encouraged to discuss options for the future rather than be told what is best for them (Bradley, 2012).

It is essential for the learner to be supported through transition, particularly early transitions. Incidence of school refusal is highest in children aged five and six years (Ollendick and Mayer, 1984, cited in Giallo et al, 2010) therefore it is essential that mechanisms be put in place to ensure transitions are effective from the beginning. Key to this is listening to the learner's voice and supporting those in the learner's microsystem.

Stakeholders (parents and caregivers)

While an individual experiences the transition, those closest to them also experience elements of the same transition process. Key stakeholders (parents and caregivers) are a key part of the child's microsystem so when the child transitions to a new setting, the stakeholders become part of a wider system. New relationships are formed and existing relationships change, so that it is not only children that experience transition. Stakeholders might need to be supported in order to help them cope with the change. An approach to support stakeholders to understand the challenges of transition and impact on the learners is to create a community of practice which is a network of connections between stakeholders and schools.

However, the role of key stakeholders – such as parents, caregivers or partners – in facilitating the experiences of transition must not be overlooked. These individuals can play a key role in the success of the transition experience because they are the constant factor in the individual's life throughout the period of change (O'Toole et al, 2014). It is important, therefore, that they also have a voice, and are involved in the facilitation of the transition experience. A research study in the UK by Zeedyk et al (2003) found that while key stakeholders were *'well informed as to children's expectations'* (ibid, p 71) of transition, more attention needed to be focused upon their roles.

WHY IT IS IMPORTANT TO INCLUDE KEY STAKEHOLDERS

There is little evidence that the support for key stakeholders is a consideration in the wider planning for transition (NFER, 2006), despite research clearly demonstrating the impact the child's microsystem has upon educational attainment and aspiration (Østergaard Larsen et al, 2014; Kaplun et al, 2017). Bronfenbrenner's (1979) ecological systems theory states that when there are changes to the learner's mesosystem there are also developmental changes and expectations in behaviour associated with that change. However, key stakeholders are often left on the periphery of this mesosystem and typically are only given information rather than required to be actively involved in discussion around the processes and potential challenges that learners could face (Giallo et al, 2010). Descriptions of the transition process by stakeholders in a study by O'Toole et al (2014) noted that it was an intense and emotional time for them. Some commented that they had a sense of alienation, as their children became more independent, and the approach of the school with regards to stakeholders was less inclusive. However, the role of key stakeholders is critical in imparting knowledge and attitudes to the learner and should not be overlooked as the connections between the home and the setting shape children's educational trajectories (Moorman Kim et al, 2012). Parental involvement and attitude towards the education of their child has been found to affect engagement and performance (Kaplun et al, 2017; Petrakos and Lehrer, 2011). Socioeconomic factors such as parental education, occupational status, family income and family structure all play an important part. According to Østergaard Larsen et al (2014) there are correlations with socioeconomic and social factors. Learners from favourable socioeconomic backgrounds are more likely to achieve academic success and to find employment than those from lower socioeconomic status. In fact, the impact of disadvantage is far reaching, influencing interactions within the learner's mesosystem as well as impacting upon parenting and family relationships. These disruptions in Bronfenbrenner's (1979) lower-order systems (microsystems and mesosystems) become compounded and can impact on the quality of the transition experience for the learner.

Engagement with the key stakeholders is therefore fundamentally important to ensure successful transitions. McIntyre et al (2007) found that early involvement by stakeholders in initial transition experiences has an influence on future transitional experiences. Families of young children were asked what activities or services they had in relation to transition, what they wanted and what they neither had nor wanted. The findings from the study suggested that stakeholders wanted more information about the transition process, including behavioural and academic expectations around the new setting; contact with the new practitioner; and information on how they could prepare the learner for entry to the new setting. As McIntyre et al (2007, p 86) note, *'parents' motivation to participate in transition planning represents an opportunity to create important family-school partnerships'*. However, parents are often unsure about how to become involved in the process and of their role. Providing a solid foundation for the transition process is essential because the older the learners become the more distanced stakeholders are from the transitional process. There are also increasing demands upon the learner to become more autonomous. This is particularly evident as the learner enters higher education, for example, where the focus is on independent learning and effective approaches to academic work (Postareff et al, 2017). Therefore, a key role for stakeholders early on is to equip learners with the necessary skills and knowledge to cope with change and increasing demands to become independent.

UNDERSTANDING THE RELATIONSHIP BETWEEN KEY STAKEHOLDERS, LEARNERS AND PRACTITIONERS

Interactions between the microsystem and the mesosystem influence the social pathways of the learner, especially during times of transition in early life (Elder Jr et al, 2003) and connect to life-course theory. Life-course theory proposes that the length of time between transitions (known as durations) can be beneficial in supporting behavioural stability. Preparing for transition before it begins gives learners and key stakeholders time to adjust to change as their lives are lived interdependently (Elder Jr et al, 2003). Improving communication in the mesosystem could alleviate concerns of both learners and key stakeholders alike. This supports Vygotsky's (1978) sociocultural theory in identifying the significance of social interaction in the development of cognition. Meaningful interaction between key stakeholders and practitioners means the experiences of transition for all involved could be organised and experienced more effectively. Schools can set up communities of practice with their stakeholders to share experience. Lave and Wenger (1991) suggest three components of a community of practice to support the sharing of knowledge and experience. This could be applied in the following way to manage the transition experience:

- **domain of interest**: supporting learners at different transition points;
- **community**: activities to share expertise and experience to help each other;
- **practice**: practitioners sharing knowledge of their experience in the classroom.

Despite the fact it is recognised that the relationship between key stakeholders and practitioners is vital for effective transitions, O'Toole et al (2014, p 122) note the partnership between the two may be difficult since *'parents are a far from homogenous group'*. In addition, stakeholders may feel unprepared for the transition process and unsure of how to provide appropriate support for the learner. However stakeholders understanding the process of transition and realising its significance from the earliest stages is vital in order to influence effective change (Kaplun et al, 2017). In this context, duration becomes important. A 2016 study by Neal et al found that interventions to support the transition process were more effective when they were longer in duration. This gave learners (and stakeholders) time to adjust to the change and meant the interventions were more appropriate to their developmental needs.

Practitioners

A buoyant interconnected relationship between practitioners, stakeholders and learners is fundamental in ensuring that all parties are involved in transition arrangements involving the learner. Practitioners play a key role in ensuring successful transition (Skouteris et al, 2012). They are responsible for commencing the transition process and key in its facilitation and organisation. Therefore it is imperative that there are clear communication channels between school and home around transition, as Schwartz et al (2006, p 89) state, 'communication between educators and families is key, not only to information-sharing but in the creation and improvement of successful participation in adult life'.

THE IMPORTANCE OF HOME-SCHOOL RELATIONSHIPS

Effective home–school communication ensures that stakeholders are able to guide and direct learners in accordance with the educational setting's transitional procedures and serves to minimise potential concern and possible anxiety among learners. The acknowledgement of the fundamental role of communication between home and school supports Bronfenbrenner's (1979) ecological systems theory. An effective relationship within the learner's mesosystem allows for an increased awareness of how the learner is responding to the transition process in a number of contexts. It also enables practitioners to tailor approaches centred on the learner's needs. However, often practitioners express mixed opinions of the exact role parents should play within the educational context and how congruent the messages are between home and school (Petrakos and Lehrer, 2011). It appears that while there is an emphasis on shared meaning created to support the individual's learning, often there is a challenge as to how that is most effectively communicated by practitioners. Parameters for stakeholder involvement need to be made clear to all parties involved. However, these can vary considerably according to practitioner approach potentially making the navigation of communication by stakeholders with the educational setting difficult.

While there may be a lack of clarity around roles, practitioners can often find it difficult to develop effective communication pathways with the home. This can be due to a number of reasons, including stakeholders' prior negative schooling experiences or issues with language (O'Toole et al, 2014). In this way the impact of the stakeholders' life trajectories and their own experiences influence that of the learner (Hutchison, 2011). Strategies to overcome such barriers can include providing opportunities for parents to enter the school for informal events such as coffee mornings, or to participate in activities with their children. Schwartz et al (2006) point out that the literature often discusses involving learners and including parents for successful transition, but what is often not documented is how professionals such as practitioners and multi-agency professionals receive and disseminate critical information from these encounters. While there is an acknowledgement of the importance of interconnected and interdependent relationships between learner, practitioner, stakeholder and the wider community, it is often not structured or documented clearly, particularly in the discussions around transition (Petrakos and Lehrer, 2011). Often boundaries are unclear and can merge or diverge thus impacting upon the fluidity of the transition.

DEVELOPING EFFECTIVE RELATIONSHIPS

All relationships (eg between learners and their peers between learners and stakeholders, and between practitioners at different levels and between educational settings) play a central role in effective educational transitions (O'Toole et al, 2014). This is evidence of Bronfenbrenner's ecological systems theory (1979) theory concerning the effect of relationships and interactions between levels (mesosystem and exosystem). However, for the practitioner, knowing the learner in the transition process is critical. Peters (2010, p 2) states,

children, whose teachers take time to get to know them, affirm their culture, recognise and build on their prior learning, and see promise rather than deficits, reflect many of the features of a successful transition that will support their learning.

By knowing the learners well, practitioners can tailor transitional preparations and experiences to the individual need of the learner. By doing so, the practitioner adopts the life-course perspective in considering the diverse context of some learners and its potential impact upon transition (Hutchison, 2011).

MANAGING CHANGE

As well as forming meaningful relationships, practitioners need to support learners appropriately for the changing academic expectations between different educational contexts (O'Toole et al, 2014). However, Stephen and Cope (2003, p 262) found that teachers of children entering primary schooling saw transition

as a one-way process in which children had to 'fit in' to school, and did not see it as their task to respond to the diversity of the children's preferences, previous experiences or background.

While practitioners in the study acknowledged that some learners had more difficulty in adjusting following the transition, there was little evidence that they adapted their practice in response. This seems to go against Vygotsky's (1978) sociocultural theory, that it is the practitioner's role to scaffold the transition experience.

Failure to ensure a successful transition can lead to a delay in learning as recognised by both the Department for Children, Schools and Families (DCSF) (2009) and the Welsh Assembly Government in their report, *Exploring Education Transitions for Pupils aged 6–8 in Wales* (Morris et al, 2010). This was particularly relevant for learners from lower socioeconomic backgrounds, for whom a negative experience of transition can lead to a lack of progress or even impede learning in the new setting. According to life-course theory the impact of one experience can influence the individual's course of action when faced with similar situations (Hutchison, 2011), and therefore a negative experience of one transition can permeate and affect other transitions.

SUCCESSFUL TRANSITION OPPORTUNITIES

To ensure good transitions, Cassidy (2005) suggests providing opportunities for cross-phase communication between practitioners to share information about learners. How this is achieved needs to be reviewed and improved with a suggestion that practitioners should experiment with different techniques and not be afraid to acknowledge failure, in order to ensure an effective transitional experience (Morris et al, 2010). Skouteris et al (2012), among others, suggest that practitioners need to ensure that collaboration during the cross-phase communication process considers how learners will cope with potentially different pedagogies – for example the anxiety of moving from play-based learning to something more structured (Margetts, 2002). Einarsdóttir et al (2008) claim this is not done. In fact, research suggests practitioners in primary and secondary schools know very little about each other's work, and seek to find out from the learner, rather than each other (O'Toole et al, 2014). This reflects Bronfenbrenner's (1979) ecological systems theory, which argues that the individual's chronosystems are potentially affected by limited interactions between identified systems. However, effective cross-phase collaboration requires funding (Boyle and Petriwskyj, 2014). In Wales, the emergence of the Curriculum Pioneer Model is predicated on a model of collaboration, whereby educational settings work together to design and develop the new curriculum (Donaldson, 2015). Even though the focus and purpose of the current model is not on transition, increased collaboration and communication between practitioners can only serve to enhance discussions around the operational mechanisms of transition.

Enhanced cross-phase communication supports the maintenance of continuity which is an important element of transition. While recognising that change is a key factor in the transition process, it is important that, where possible, elements of continuity are preserved. Where there are familiarities in the new environment, learners are able to ally previously learned skills and knowledge; however, as Skouteris et al (2012, p 79) state, *'the more differences between the two environments, the more challenges and stress'* are faced by the learner during the transition. Skouteris et al (2012) suggest that these discontinuities are often as a result of existing policies and frameworks and not individual teachers. For example, Fisher (2009) identifies the marked difference in pedagogical focus and lack of continuity between the child-centred focused Foundation Stage curriculum and subsequent Key Stage 1 curriculum, where the focus is more upon academic practice and success. According to Margetts (2002) continuity can be achieved through organised operational mechanisms: the more planned transition activities the better the continuity. This recognises the interactions between the individual's microsystems with each other, thus developing the mesosystem (Bronfenbrenner, 1979).

PLANNING FOR TRANSITION

While transition programmes need to be flexible in order to understand individual concerns and to address them appropriately, there is a general agreement that transition programmes and activities should take place days or weeks before the change takes place and even throughout the year in order to fully prepare the learner (Zeedyk et al, 2003). Indeed, Ahtola et al (2011, p 299) suggest that *'the greater the variety of transition practices implemented by teachers, the more the children's skills develop',* and the better prepared they are in making the move from one educational level to the next. Life-course theory suggests that appreciation of human agency, and providing opportunities for learners to process change, supports the effective implementation of the transition process

(Hutchison, 2011). This is further supported by Smith (2002), who investigated transition between preschool and primary playgrounds and found that children who were supported socially and emotionally before the transition developed a sense of belonging. The learners supported each other so that when they started at the new setting, they were more resilient to the change and formed more friendships.

INCLUDING THE LEARNER VOICE

Having an understanding and being aware of learners' concerns and questions about forthcoming transitions is essential for ensuring a positive experience for learners with additional needs. It is important to have a team of multi-professionals and a transition plan to support them (Schwartz et al, 2006). This means being able to mitigate the impact of transition, which can significantly improve the learner's experience of change and ensure continuity between one educational level and the next. Jindal-Snape and Miller (2008) found that a learner's social and emotional well-being is enhanced when educators fully understand transition, and yet

---

teachers rarely identified children's individual abilities as making a difference to the transition process, focusing instead on institutional initiatives, an emphasis that carries the risk of creating a degree of helplessness for individual pupils.

(Zeedyk et al, 2003, p 67)

Not involving learners in the transition process can create a feeling of disempowerment that the transition is being done to them rather than being an integral part of the process.

A key barrier to practitioners being able to support future transitions is a lack of information about the next stage. For example, for learners with additional needs moving out of school, practitioners felt they could not support the transition effectively because they were not *'specialists in adult services'* and therefore students' futures may be compromised (Schwartz et al, 2006, p 89). This means practitioners must strive to have an understanding of the next step so that they can ensure that learners are equipped with the necessary skills and knowledge to adapt.

Recommendations

According to O'Toole et al (2014) concerns about transition are similar regardless of the age or the experiences of the learner. Many settings have structured transition practices to support the process for learners. Some of the more common transition practices involve visits prior to the learner starting at the new setting and open evenings. Practices such as shortening the school day, staggered entry and home visits are less common (Petrakos and Lehrer, 2011).

Conclusion

Transition is an important element of an individual's journey when moving from one educational level to the next. To better understand the complexities of transition it is useful to frame the process using theoretical perspectives. Five key theories have been used here to support understanding. Bronfenbrenner's (1979) ecological systems theory helps understand the significance of relationships and importance of interaction. This is further developed through an understanding of Vygotsky's (1978) sociocultural theory of cognitive development, and life-course theory developed by Hutchison (2011). The communities of practice theory as developed by Lave and Wenger (1991) supports collaboration between practitioners in facilitating the transition process while van Gennep's (2019) theory acknowledges that the transition process is a natural part of development. Each theory helps inform knowledge about the place and role of learner, the key stakeholders (those closest to the learner) and practitioners in transition.

❖ Reflective questions

1. What have you learnt about the five theoretical frameworks?

2. Using your understanding of the frameworks, what are the main barriers to effective transitions?

3. How does knowing about theoretical frameworks help support effective transitions?

4. When preparing for transition, what considerations should be taken into account?

5. What is your role in preparing for transition?

Suggested reading

1. **Aubrey, K and Riley, A (2017)** *Understanding and Using Challenging Educational Theories*. **London: Sage.**

This book gives a comprehensive overview of a selection of key thinkers who have offered challenging perspectives on education some of which can be applied to experiences of transition.

2. **Symonds, J (2015)** *Understanding School Transitions: What Happens to Children and How to Help Them*. **London: Routledge.**

This book provides practical advice for practitioners in supporting learners during periods of transition.

3. Rae, T (2014) *Supporting Successful Transition from Primary to Secondary School (Programme for Teachers).* London: Routledge.

Acknowledging that transition from primary to secondary school can be a stressful experience, this book explains how to support learners during the process to ensure a successful and smooth transition.

References

Ackesjö, H (2013) Children Crossing Borders: School Visits as Initial Incorporation Rites in Transition to Preschool Class. *International Journal of Early Childhood*, 45: 387–410. [online] Available at: https://doi.org/10.1007/s13158-013-0080-7 (accessed 13 June 2020).

Ahtola, A, Silinskas, G, Poikonen, P, Kontoniemi, M, Niemi, P and Nurmi, J (2011) Transition to Formal Schooling: Do Transition Practices Matter for Academic Performance? *Early Childhood Research Quarterly*, 26: 295–302. [online] Available at: https://doi.org/10.1016/j.ecresq.2010.12.002 (accessed 13 June 2020).

Boyle, T and Petriwskyj, A (2014) Transitions to School: Reframing Professional Relationships. *Early Years*, 34(4): 392–404. [online] Available at: https://doi.org/10.1080/09575146.2014.953042 (accessed 7 June 2020).

Bradley, J (2012) Young People Navigating the Transition to University: Policy, Context and Influences. *Educational & Child Psychology*, 29(1): 101–10.

Bronfenbrenner, U (1979) *The Ecology of Human Development: Experiments by Nature and Design*. Boston, MA: Harvard University Press.

Cassidy, M (2005) 'They Do It Anyways': A Study of Primary 1 Teachers' Perceptions of Children's Transition Into Primary Education. *Early Years*, 25: 143–53. [online] Available at: https://doi.org/10.1080/09575140500127923 (accessed 7 June 2020).

Department for Children, Schools and Families (2009) Deprivation and Education: The Evidence on Pupils in England, Foundation Stage to Key Stage 4. [online] Available at: https://dera.ioe.ac.uk/9431/1/DCSF-RTP-09-01.pdf (accessed 7 June 2020).

Di Santo, A and Berman, R (2012) Beyond the Preschool Years: Children's Perceptions About Starting Kindergarten. *Children & Society*, 26: 469–79. [online] Available at: https://doi.org/10.1111/j.1099-0860.2011.00360.x (accessed 7 June 2020).

Donaldson, G (2015) Successful Futures. Independent Review of Curriculum and Assessment Arrangements in Wales. [online] Available at: https://dera.ioe.ac.uk/22165/2/150225-successful-futures-en_Redacted.pdf (accessed 7 June 2020).

Einarsdóttir, J, Perry, B and Dockett, S (2008) Transition to School Practices: Comparisons From Iceland and Australia. *Early Years*, 28(1): 47–60. [online] Available at: https://doi.org/10.1080/09575140801924689 (accessed 7 June 2020).

Elder Jr, G H, Johnson, M K and Crosnoe, R (2003) The Emergence and Development of Life Course Theory. In Mortimer, J T and Shanahan, M J (2003) (eds) *Handbook of the Life Course*. New York: Kluwer Academic/Plenum Publishers.

Fisher, J (2009) 'We Used to Play in Foundation, It Was More Funner': Investigating Feelings About Transition From Foundation Stage to Year 1. *Early Years*, 29: 131–45. [online] Available at: https://doi.org/10.1080/09575140802672576 (accessed 7 June 2020).

Galton, M and McLellan, R (2018) A Transition Odyssey: Pupils' Experiences of Transfer to Secondary School Across Five Decades. *Research Papers in Education*, 33(2): 255–77. [online] Available at: https://doi.org/10.1080/02671522.2017.1302496 (accessed 7 June 2020).

Giallo, R, Treyvaud, K, Matthews, J and Kienhuis, M (2010) Making the Transition to Primary School: An Evaluation of a Transition Program for Parents. *Australian Journal of Educational and Developmental Psychology*, 10: 1–17.

Gouthro, P (2019) Taking Time to Learn: The Importance of Theory for Adult Education. *Education Quarterly*, 69(1): 60–76. [online] Available at: https://doi.org/10.1177/0741713618815656 (accessed 7 June 2020).

Hugo, K, McNamara, K, Sheldon, K, Moult, F, Lawrence, K, Forbes, C, Martin, N and Miller, M (2018) Developing a Blueprint for Action on the Transition to School: Implementation of an Action Research Project within a Preschool Community. *International Journal of Early Childhood*, 50(2): 241–57. [online] Available at: https://doi.org/10.1007/s13158-018-0220-1 (accessed 7 June 2020).

Hutchison, E D (2011) Life Course Theory. In Levesque, R J R (ed) *Encyclopaedia of Adolescence*. New York, NY: Springer.

Jindal-Snape, D and Miller, D J (2008) A Challenge of Living? Understanding the Psycho-social Processes of the Child During Primary-Secondary Transition Through Resilience and Self-Esteem Theories. *Educational Psychology Review*, 20: 217–36.

Kaplun, C, Dockett, S and Perry, B (2017) The Starting School Study: Mothers' Perspectives of Transition to School. *Australasian Journal of Early Childhood*, 42(4): 56–66. [online] Available at: https://doi.org/10.23965/AJEC.42.4.07 (accessed 7 June 2020).

Lave, J and Wenger, E (1991) *Situated Learning: Legitimate Peripheral Participation*. Cambridge, UK: Cambridge University Press.

Loizou, E (2011) Empowering Aspects of Transition From Kindergarten to First Grade Through Children's Voices. *Early Years*, 31(1): 43–55. [online] Available at: https://doi.org/10.1080/09575146.2010.515943 (accessed 7 June 2020).

MacDonald, A (2009) Drawing Stories: The Power of Children's Drawings to Communicate the Lived Experience of Starting School. *Australasian Journal of Early Childhood*, 34(2): 40–9. [online] Available at: https://doi.org/10.1177/183693910903400306 (accessed 7 June 2020).

Margetts, K (2002) Transition to School - Complexity and Diversity. *European Early Childhood Education Research Journal*, 10(2): 103–14. [online] Available at: https://doi.org/10.1080/13502930285208981 (accessed 7 June 2020).

McIntyre, L L, Eckert, T L, Fiese, B H, DiGennaro, F D and Wildenger, L K (2007) Transition to Kindergarten: Family Experiences and Involvement. *Early Childhood Education Journal*, 35(1): 83–8. [online] Available at: https://doi.org/10.1007/s10643-007-0175-6 (accessed 7 June 2020).

McPhail, R (2015) Pre-University Prepared Students: A Programme for Facilitating the Transition From Secondary to Tertiary Education. *Teaching in Higher Education*, 20(6): 652–65. [online] Available at: https://doi.org/10.1080/13562517.2015.1062360 (accessed 7 June 2020).

Moorman Kim, E, Coutts, M J, Holmes, S R, Sheridan, S M, Ransom, K A, Sjuts, T M and Rispoli, K M (2012) Parent Involvement and Family–School Partnerships: Examining the Content, Processes, and Outcomes of Structural Versus Relationship-based Approaches. CYFS Working Paper No. 2012-6. [online] Available at: www.cyfs.unl.edu/resources/downloads/working-papers/CYFS_Working_Paper_2012_6.pdf (accessed 7 June 2020).

Morris, M, McCrindle, L, Cheung, J, Johnson, R, Pietikainen, A and Smith, R (2010) *Exploring Education Transitions for Pupils Aged 6–8 in Wales*. [online] Available at: http://sqw.co.uk/files/8513/8523/9982/CYP8.pdf (accessed 7 June 2020).

Neal, S, Rice, F, Ng-Knight, T, Riglin, L and Frederickson, N (2016) Exploring the Longitudinal Association between Interventions to Support the Transition to Secondary School and Child Anxiety. *Journal of Adolescence*, 50: 31–43. [online] Available at: https://doi.org/10.1016/j.adolescence.2016.04.003 (accessed 13 June 2020).

NFER (2006) Transition from Primary to Secondary School: Current Arrangements and Good Practice in Wales. Final Report. [online] Available at: https://nfer.ac.uk/media/2243/wtn01.pdf (accessed 7 June 2020).

OECD (2017) *Starting Strong V: Transitions From Early Childhood Education and Care to Primary Education*. Paris: OECD Publishing. [online] Available at: https://doi.org/10.1787/9789264276253-en (accessed 7 June 2020).

Østergaard Larsen, B, Jensen, L and Pilegaard Jensen, T (2014) Transitions in Secondary Education: Exploring the Effects of Social Problems. *Research in Social Stratification and Mobility*, 38: 32–42. [online] Available at: https://doi.org/10.1016/j.rssm.2014.05.001 (accessed 7 June 2020).

O'Toole, L, Hayes, N and Mhic Mhathúna, M (2014) A Bio-Ecological Perspective on Educational Transition. *Social and Behavioral Sciences*, 140: 121–7. [online] Available at: https://doi.org/10.21427/D7GP4Z (accessed 7 June 2020).

Perry, B and Dockett, S (2011) 'How 'bout We Have a Celebration!' Advice From Children on Starting School. *European Early Childhood Education Research Journal*, 19(3): 373–86. [online] Available at: https://doi.org/10.1080/1350293X.2011.597969 (accessed 7 June 2020).

Peters, S (2010) *Literature Review: Transition from Early Childhood Education to School*. New Zealand: Ministry of Education.

Petrakos, H and Lehrer, J (2011) Parents' and Teachers' Perceptions of Transition Practices in Kindergarten. *Exceptionality Education International*, 21(2): 62–73.

Postareff, L, Mattsson, M, Lindblom-Ylanne, S and Hailikari, T (2017) The Complex Relationship Between Emotions, Approaches to Learning, Study Success and Study Progress During the Transition to University. *Higher Education*, 73: 441–57. [online] Available at: https://doi.org/10.1007/s10734-016-0096-7 (accessed 7 June 2020).

Schwartz, K, Mactavish, J and Lutfiyya, Z (2006) Making Community Connections: Educator Perspectives on Transition Planning for Students With Intellectual Disabilities. *Exceptionality Education Canada*, 16(2): 73–100.

Skouteris, H, Watson, B and Lum, J (2012) Preschool Children's Transition to Formal Schooling: The Importance of Collaboration Between Teachers, Parents and Children. *Australasian Journal of Early Childhood*, 37(4): 78–85.

Smith, N (2002) Transition to the School Playground: An Intervention Programme for Nursery Children. *Early Years*, 22(2): 129–46.

Stephen, C and Cope, P (2003) An Inclusive Perspective to Transition to Primary School. *European Educational Research Journal*, 2(2): 262–76. [online] Available at: https://doi.org/10.2304/eerj.2003.2.2.5 (accessed 7 June 2020).

UNICEF UK (1989) Conventions on the Rights of the Child. [online] Available at: https://unicef.org.uk/wp-content/uploads/2010/05/UNCRC_united_nations_convention_on_the_rights_of_the_child.pdf (accessed 7 June 2020).

van Gennep, A (2019) *The Rites of Passage* (second edition). Chicago: University of Chicago Press.

Vygotsky, L (1978) *Mind in Society. The Development of Higher Psychological Processes*. Cambridge, MA: Harvard University Press.

Waller, T (2009) Modern Childhood: Contemporary Theories and Children's Lives. In Waller, T (ed) *An Introduction to Early Childhood*. London: SAGE Publications Ltd.

Wenger, E (1998) *Communities of Practice: Learning, Meaning and Identity*. Cambridge University Press. [online] Available at: https://psycnet.apa.org/doi/10.1017/CBO9780511803932 (accessed 7 June 2020).

Zeedyk, S M, Gallacher, J, Henderson, M, Hope, G, Husband, B and Lindsay, K (2003) Negotiating the Transition from Primary to Secondary School: Perceptions of Pupils, Parents and Teachers. *School Psychology International*, 24: 67–79. [online] Available at: https://doi.org/10.1177/0143034303024001010 (accessed 7 June 2020).

3. VULNERABLE TRANSITIONS

Recap

Chapter 2 explored how theoretical perspectives can frame and support understanding of transition. The theories investigated were examined through three lenses:

1. the learner who experiences the transition;
2. the key stakeholders who support the learner;
3. the practitioners who instigate and facilitate the transition process.

These theories enable a better understanding of the interdependency of all involved, and how the transition process affects them both as individuals and collectively. This is essential for ensuring that the experience is a positive one. Framing the transition process using theory enables the creation of a holistic framework from which to develop a coherent approach to the understanding of transition. This serves to ensure the achievement of effective experiences of transition.

Rationale

Times of change in education have an impact upon all children and young people but for some individuals and groups the effect prior to and post transition can be even greater. Compulsory education 'batches' learners according to age rather than stage of learning and this is reflected in transition policies. This chapter will explore the impact that transition may have for learners identified under the Equality Act (UK Government, 2010) as being vulnerable. This includes learners who are refugees, asylum seekers, traveller children, children with identity and gender questions and children with disabilities. There is clear evidence that these children require additional support particularly when adapting from one educational setting to another, even though they are not considered to have special educational needs (SEN), additional learning needs (ALN) in Wales or additional support needs (ASN) in Scotland (DfE, 2018; NASEN, 2014). Difficulty in adapting could be due to factors such as adverse childhood experiences (ACEs), or due to cultural, social and language differences (Sutherland et al, 2010).

Understanding terminology

Due to the wide remit encompassed by the term vulnerable, this chapter will use the term SEN while also acknowledging that learners' support requirements are individual and that this should be a fundamental consideration in any transition process. The variety of factors that may result in a learner having SEN provides justification that the level and type of support received during transition is based according to individual need. The Special Educational Needs and Disability Code of Practice (Department for Education and Department for Health, 2015, p 19) states:

Local Authorities must ensure that children, young people and parents are provided with the information, advice and support necessary to enable them to participate in discussions and decisions about their support.

This suggests that the process needs to be a holistic one whereby the learner and parents or caregiver are part of the process. It is also important to appreciate that key stakeholders involved in the learner's transition process may be vulnerable too. This should be taken into account when preparing learners for transition ensuring that good communication is maintained and that a consistent approach is taken between settings and stakeholders (NASEN, 2014). As a representation of the numbers of children identified with SEN, in 2019 14.6 per cent of learners in England were identified as having SEN, equating to 1.3 million pupils (DfE, 2019). This is an increase in numbers since 2017. Despite the significance of these figures, it is interesting to note that few studies have investigated the impact of transition upon learners with SEN despite an increase in the number of learners receiving additional support (Hughes et al, 2013).

While analogies can be drawn with the experiences of learners who are not considered vulnerable or who do not have SEN, it is important that there is a parity of experience for all learners undergoing transition to the same setting. Evidence shows that the social, emotional or academic needs of learners with SEN can be intensified through the transition process (Hebron, 2017). It is important therefore to consider the type of need and support required by the individual learner. A study by Kvalsund and Bele (2010) found that the quality of an individual's social capital plays an integral part in determining the success of transition for young people with SEN, particularly when leaving compulsory education and entering work life. This supports Bronfenbrenner's (1979) ecological systems theory, which asserts that the reciprocal interaction of multiple systems influences a child's cognitive development and behaviour. Providing a framework of support from one area of transition to another enables individuals to develop resilience which has longer-term consequences in terms of being able to accommodate change (Rice et al, 2015). Involvement and co-operation with others may elicit recognition and positive reinforcing reactions and self-advocacy (Bunn et al, 2017). This is particularly important when considering that pupils with SEN account for just under half of all permanent exclusions and fixed period exclusions in England (DfE, 2019). Understanding how resilience can be enhanced among vulnerable groups is key to supporting the development of skills thus empowering individuals to adapt to new situations effectively.

A range of voices contribute to the discussion in this chapter: the voices of learners considered vulnerable, their parents or caregivers, and those working with learners in educational settings, both in SEN and in mainstream settings. In addressing the needs of vulnerable learners during transition, the following areas were considered:

- preparation – how learners with SEN prepare and are prepared for transition;
- process – what happens during the process of transition for learners with SEN;
- outcome – how learners with SEN adjust and become settled in the new setting.

Transition experiences

Transition experiences in education involve both continuity and change. For those with SEN additional support may be necessary for engagement with the process, particularly in the negotiation of new practices and expectations. Relationships are critical in providing a context for educational transitions as *'people and their individual characteristics, their ways of interacting and communication, elements of different situations, and elements of time, entwine in new environments'* (Dockett and Perry, 2016, p 311). In preparing pupils for the change ahead, the role of key stakeholders in supporting the learner is significant, particularly for learners with SEN as they tend to be more reliant on parents or carers for longer than their peers (Doyle et al, 2017). Ensuring parental support works in tandem with practitioners is key to ensure successful transition. As Flitcroft and Kelly (2016, p 302) note,

how a move proceeds and develops ultimately influences its success rather than the move itself, with positive outcomes being linked to the ethos of the school and pupils feeling they were genuinely cared about, wanted, listened to and supported.

Understanding the needs of the learner and developing a coherent and cohesive approach tailored to support the transition is essential for a successful transition process.

The role of the practitioner in preparing the learner for transition

Practitioners working with learners with SEN know the importance of preparing learners for a smooth transition (Hughes et al, 2013). Usually apprehension around transition represents *'a normative and short-lived response that is generally accompanied by a sense of optimism about moving into a new school environment'* (Neal et al, 2016, p 31). Central to the concerns of learners during experiences of transition are meeting new people, workload and becoming familiar with new routines and environment (Bloyce and Frederickson, 2012). Developing good relationships, understanding the needs of the learner and listening to the learner voice are key elements central to ensuring a successful transition facilitated by practitioners. This is important not only from a psychosocial perspective but also to mitigate the potential *'attainment dip'* that often occurs during periods of transition (Bloyce and Frederickson, 2012).

Setting collaboration and co-operation

The Special Educational Needs Co-ordinator (SENCo), or in Wales, the Additional Learning Needs Co-ordinator (ALNCo), is usually the key individual involved in either arranging or facilitating transition activities for learners with SEN in both primary and secondary school settings. SENCo will be the term used in this chapter for consistency. These activities are in addition to mainstream transition activities and acknowledge that one transition approach may not suit all learners, as identified by life-course theory (Hutchison, 2011). Initial preparation for transition occurs during the final year of the learner at the setting, particularly when the learner is moving from one setting to another.

- *At Easter, [Year 6] primary teachers in the feeder schools collect data about individuals in the classes, discuss ability, interests, traits, history, needs, safeguarding... it helps us to get to know the children. For children with ALN there is a booklet for each teacher* (HoY, secondary school 1).
- *We have frequent meetings with cluster primary SENCos to discuss the needs of children coming to the school* (SENCo, secondary school 2).
- *The college has links with all the secondary schools (in the area)... and we also work with learners who may be home educated, on Local Authority tuition or come from Special Schools* (SENCo, FE college 3).
- *We have partnerships with other schools when it comes to options. Some come to us to do catering for two years and join the sixth form, our students can go to the school next door [mainstream secondary school] for A levels* (HKS4, special school 1).

Collaboration between practitioners not only enables improved perceptions of the needs of the learner on entering the transition phase but also facilitates the working approaches between settings thus enabling the development of a holistic, tailored approach to transition as identified by the communities of practice theory (Lave and Wenger, 1990). Estyn, the inspection body for Wales, in identifying good practice notes that a significant element in effective transition processes is the *'close collaborative working between schools and settings that enables them to share information about pupils with SEN'* (Estyn, 2020, p 4). For learners with SEN this can mean an extended programme of transition activities, which also may include multi-agency collaboration and planning for the transition on an individual level. On entering formal education, this can also include practitioners visiting the child at home as this can provide an opportunity for the parent to share information in an environment which is familiar to both parent and learner. This allows the practitioner to see the learner operating in an environment in which they feel comfortable and for an opportunity to gain an insight into the learner's stage of learning and development. As Morgan et al (2014, p 149) note, this can be a complex process, not only for *'reasons of personnel preparation but also for delineation of roles and responsibilities'* as the learner begins to navigate their way in the receiving setting.

Working with parents

Working with and involving parents in the transition process is critical as noted by Hirano et al (2016), who acknowledge the positive impact such collaboration has upon the holistic development of the individual in terms of engagement and achievement. This is particularly true for learners who have SEN. This is further supported by practitioners who when asked about the transition activities that they arrange for learners included parents as an integral part of their planning.

- *We meet with the most needy children and parents regularly during Years 5 and 6 and organise extended transition sessions, for example vising the school when it's quiet... They can come and visit the site as many times as they like to see the teaching rooms and have sessions in the [well-being area]* (SENCo, secondary school 2).

- *The Special Needs Resource Base meets with parents before they [learner] starts school and devise a new School Action Plan. Regular visits are planned with Teacher Assistant support for the pupil...* (SEN teacher 1).

As Estyn (2020, p 19) notes, *'where there are strong relationships with parents and families, pupils benefit from a shared understanding of what is important for the child'.* Very often parental concerns can appear greater than the worries of the learner.

- *For a lot of parents transition causes them more anxiety than it does the children* (HKS4, special school 1).

This supports Bronfenbrenner's (1979, p 6) ecological systems theory around the broadening of environments as the learner moves from one setting to another in an *'ecological transition'.* As parents or caregivers are aware of potential vulnerabilities in the learner, they may be more protective and have more concerns around the transition process than perhaps the learners themselves.

Demonstrating flexibility in providing opportunities for learners to visit the setting enables learners to begin to visualise themselves as part of that setting. Parental involvement in this process can serve to facilitate the transition. While the arrangements are more structured for learners entering FE, there is clear engagement with parents. Learners are able to visit the campus as often as they like so that they are familiar with the new environment.

- *The transition and review officer visits schools and attends the meetings of pupils with statements... They have a six-stage process which means that they will meet the student at least six times before they start college. This starts at the annual review meeting but includes a visit to the college to discuss course, to attend open evenings, to come early to registration so that they can be registered individually. Opportunities are also given for students to come and have a tour of the campus as many times as needed so that they know where facilities are before they enrol on a course and gain a familiarity with the new and often busy environment* (SENCo, FE college 3).
- *With ALN pupils the teacher often chats with parents/caregivers about how they have got on. We will then make amendments to the plan, if needed, for example making visits shorter or adding more [transition visits]* (P, Nursery/Reception 2).

For learners with more profound needs the transition is graduated, beginning in Year 9 (where appropriate) and preparing the learner for the transition to the new setting in small steps (NASEN, 2014). Often the focus is more on longer-term outcomes for learners and this guides the shorter-term transition from the special needs school to appropriate further education settings. This also involves the transition of the learner from child to adult services and discussion initially takes place in annual review meetings, where practitioners and parents can discuss options available to the learner on leaving the special needs setting. Transition events are organised annually, which include education providers, social services and options for learners. This is open to learners from Year 9 so that they have time to consider the choices available to them. This is further consolidated with meetings in Key Stage 4 and when learners are in the sixth forms when parents and pupils meet with the Head of Year. A transition officer, in conjunction with the careers officer, discusses with the learner what they would like to do and the steps that they might need to take in order to reach their goal. This is achieved through person-centred planning where the needs of the learner are taken into account.

- *We identify what they want to do and what they enjoy and also consider vocational options for them. We know them well and know what to do [to help them get there]* (Transition officer, special school 1).
- *We have a transition to adult life 14–25 plan, which is our transition protocol. We work with the local authority, health board and social services* (HKS4, special school 1).

As Lawson and Parker (2019, p 144) note, *'these principles advocate for YP [young people] and their families to have more control and choice about education'.*

Learners appreciate the support given prior to undertaking the transition process.

- *I would have struggled if I hadn't had the transition… It really helped to see the classrooms as it was a very different environment* (L1, FE college 3).
- *The College were amazing… They asked me what I would like… They try to learn from the students as well* (L3, FE college 3).

Parents likewise appreciate support.

- *It's been very helpful – we know everyone is just a phone call away if we need any help or advice or just an ear to listen* (Pt, FE college 3).
- *It wasn't so scary starting comp* (Pt, secondary school 2).
- *Good opportunities to ask any questions* (Pt, secondary school 2).
- *A superb experience of transition from mainstream secondary to [special school 1]… She attended every Tuesday for a year* (Pt, special school 1).

In some settings learners are given real-life experiences in preparation for transition into work. Projects in school equip learners with practical skills but this is done at the pace of the learner, under close supervision. Real-life experiences such as developing a t-shirt printing business based in the school; catering for workmen on a building site; and internships in hospital settings as evidenced in special school 1 enable learners to develop and enhance key employment skills before entering the world of work. Supported employment experiences are tailored to the need and capability of the learner with close supervision providing guidance and monitoring progress. Such experiences help learners, and parents, to understand *'what support they are likely to need to achieve their ambitions'* (NASEN, 2014, p 8).

Getting to know the learner

Person-centred planning is an essential component in the transition process, particularly for learners with SEN who may experience significant anxiety during the transition process (Neal et al, 2016). Failure to achieve a smooth transition can impact upon well-being and academic achievement. Ensuring that the learner begins to feel a part of the new setting is essential in mitigating this possibility. This can be achieved in a number of ways such as attending review meetings, completing questionnaires, being part of a question-and-answer session, and arranging opportunities to get to know the learners in less formal circumstances, such as residential visits and transition evenings. While this can be applied to all learners, it is established that learners with SEN require differentiated approaches, adapted to support their individual needs (DfE, 2014). All settings noted that they valued the importance of getting to know the learner and activities around this are useful for the learner, parent or caregiver as well as practitioner.

- *Circle times is valuable (before transition) as it gives the teacher the opportunity to put fears at bay and get to know the children* (P, Reception 2).
- *It's useful to get to know the children before the academic year so you can plan for the year ahead [eg children with SEN]* (P, secondary school 2).
- *The transition and review officer visits schools and attends the meetings of pupils with statements* (SENCo, FE college 3).
- *Pupils have an opportunity to meet staff and pupils from other schools during the Years 6 and 7 residential trip* (SENCo, secondary school 2).
- *We are lucky in school; we know our students really well and are responsive to individual need* (HKS4, special school 1).

Such experiences provide opportunities in a variety of contexts for the learner to express what their needs might be (and parent/caregiver too) but also enables practitioners to understand what their needs might be and to be prepared with appropriate strategies to support. As Neal et al (2016, p 33) note, a *'personalised approach seems particularly important given evidence indicating that children with SEN often experience a number of specific difficulties (eg lower self-esteem, social skills deficits) that are likely to influence transition outcomes'.* This ensures that all practitioners have a detailed understanding of pupils' needs before they arrive at the new setting.

The role of environment

Concerns around the new environment can be a particular area of anxiety for all learners, but in particular those who have SEN. Sutherland et al (2010, p 72) comment on moving from the primary school to secondary school that it is *'the palpable change of school culture and ethos'* as the learner is moving from an environment where they are well known by their teachers and are relatively confident in their surroundings to a larger and unfamiliar territory. This is the *'theme most frequently referred to in terms of the pupils' anxieties about transition to high school [that relates] to their "feelings" towards "change", and in particular the change in their environment, peer group, and learning'* (Bunn et al, 2017, p 241). Concerns about the environment were initial themes raised during discussion around transition, with learners at all points of transition noting that they felt *'anxious'*, *'nervous'* and *'scared of change'* about moving to the new setting although this was connected to feelings of *'excitement'* and *'anticipation'* and concerns about the layout of the new setting.

- *The one thing my son found harder than anything else was finding the right classroom – he got lost a lot* (Pt, secondary school 2).

In preparing learners for the transition, strategies implemented to alleviate extreme feelings of anxiousness include using ICT software which allows learners to virtually explore the new setting; providing opportunities for learners to visit the new setting at the end of the day or during school holidays (secondary school 2); and organising Keeping in Touch (KIT) days for learners to attend the setting during holiday periods so that they become familiar with their surroundings and key staff (FE college 3). Having a key person to liaise with during transition was found to be critical in effective transition preparations for older learners as they then already have a familiar point of reference before starting a new course. This means that the further education (FE) transition officer works closely with the school setting, first getting to know the learner in the school setting and later becoming a key figure and point of reference in the transition to FE. This supports Bronfenbrenner's (1979) ecological systems theory as elements from the old environment are familiar in the new environment and the learner is able to make that connection. Evidence from research by Rice et al (2011) found that concerns around environment and organisation reduced once learners had undergone the transition process.

Fostering a sense of belonging

Fostering a sense of belonging in the new environment is an important feature in the preparation for transition but becomes more important during the process of transition, as learners become an integral part of the receiving setting. Flitcroft and Kelly (2016, p 301) note that there is a *'growing body of evidence as a useful concept in further illuminating the nature of school contexts linked to positive pupil outcomes'*. Their findings emphasise the importance of ensuring that learners feel part of the setting, and that developing a sense of belonging in the individual can have a positive impact upon longer-term outcomes, both social and emotional as well as academic. Flitcroft and Kelly (2016) identified a number of themes central to the sense of belonging and effective engagement of learners during times of transition. These include generating a strong school identity through means such as school uniform, providing key information about the school, such as handbooks, and signposting to facilities immediately prior to transition. The comments noted below demonstrate how effective such strategies are in enabling a sense of belonging among learners.

- *We were given a book by the school. It told us about the next steps, how you can adapt to high school... I still use the book. It helped to read it before going up to the new school and gave me confidence. You know what to do if something is worrying you* (L3, secondary school 2).

- *We were given a KIT day bag with a goody bag, college handbook and then were shown around the college* (L1, FE college 3).
- *A photobook is given to ALN pupils with pictures of the classroom and teachers* (P3, Reception 2).

This arms the learner with key information about the new setting before formally starting at the new setting. Resources can be used as a point of reference or as reminder about the forthcoming change and new setting.

Establishing new social circles

While developing familiarity with the new environment is significant in the transition process, maintaining and developing new social circles is another critical factor (Neal et al, 2016). Frequent concerns expressed by learners with SEN about the transition process are a fear about being separated from current friends and the ability to make new friends.

- *Not knowing anyone… I was worried about leaving friends and the teachers… and that I wouldn't make new friends* (L1, secondary school 2).

These concerns are intertwined with other worries such as *'bullying, getting lost, an increased workload, peer relationships, and new environments and routines with fears of bulling being by far the most commonly reported concern'* (Rice et al, 2011, p 245). Practitioner awareness of these concerns is important in addressing need as poor transition experiences can have a long-term impact on the individual. This was a factor commented upon by participants.

- *School visits/lessons/activities – very useful – geographically and socially* (Pt, secondary school 2).
- *The team building activities helped… we had to think as a team or it wouldn't have worked* (L3, secondary school 2).
- *We got to know a lot of people during the transition days… enough to make friends* (L2, secondary school 2).
- *We had activities to help us settle. We planned out scenarios so that if something happened I would know what to do* (L3, FE college 3).
- *I definitely would have struggled if I hadn't had the transition* (L1, FE college 3).

It is difficult to note the potential indicators for those learners most at risk of poor transition due to the limited research available (Rice et al, 2011). However, when the transition is successful, learners, in particular older learners, are aware of this.

- *It's lot better than school. I have changed a lot since coming to college. It's a new start here… college has helped me a lot more than school* (L1, FE college 3).

- *They are supportive here. We do nice things and they give us suggestions* (L1, secondary school 2).
- *If I was to be bullied here, I would feel really supported. Before I didn't trust any teachers... but here I trust them... anyone would help. I feel very supported* (L1, FE college 3).

Providing support

While a number of settings identified a point in the transition process when they consider the learner to be assimilated and part of the new setting, for learners with SEN progression is more subtle, and allows opportunities for learners to access additional support as and when necessary. The transition process therefore needs to be flexible and reactive to individual need, as noted by practitioners working with learners with SEN.

- *The Well-being Department has a list of all children who have received ELSA [Emotional Literacy Support Assistant] intervention. A group is then set up to meet every fortnight. We have nurture clubs and a number of different interventions. Some children are more vulnerable than others. We also have a counsellor... who comes in two days a week* (HoY, secondary school 1).
- *We have a learning coach who talks with students in transition groups about any worries or concerns that they have* (Transition officer, special school 1).

Learners with SEN are monitored throughout their time in the new setting, often with informal systems in place, such as being able to access areas designated for their particular needs (eg well-being room, specialist base) and also in a more formal way.

- *When students who have a Statement of SEN attend [college], over the last two years they have been part of the trial individual development plan (IDP) process... Every week the learners are reviewed by the ALN team. They look at attendance and progression and track their progress throughout the academic year. This give the team opportunities to identify if a learner is struggling and intervention is needed to be put in place to get them back on track* (SENCo, FE college 3).

While there is an expectation that learners with SEN will assimilate and become part of the new setting in exactly the same way as all other learners there is an acknowledgement of a continuum of need and an appropriate response. As Huser et al (2016, p 445) note, *'there is no expectation that all children use the same bridge in the same ways. As well, consideration is given to how other people traverse the various bridges they meet during the transition... process'.* As the transition process is accommodated according to individual need, further support is available if required as evidenced in special school 1 where a learner returned to the setting, of her own volition, once a week in order to maintain contact and to seek reassurance.

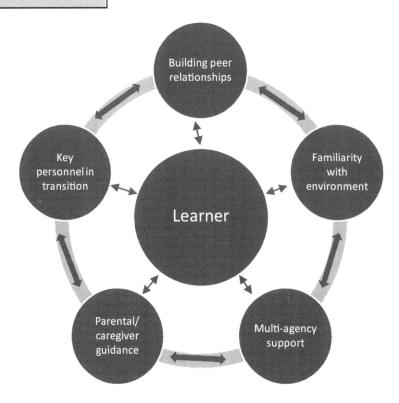

Figure 3.1 Developing a holistic approach to supporting the learner with SEN

In analysing the responses from learners, practitioners and parents/caregivers in conjunction with the literature, a number of points have been highlighted that need to be considered when planning for effective transitions for learners with SEN.

- The additional needs of individual learners should be taken into account when developing supplementary transition activities.
- The learner voice needs to be accounted for during the transition process.
- Support and guidance around transition for parents/caregivers might also need to be taken into account.
- Ensuring a successful transition has wider ramifications for the holistic development of the learner.
- Consider incorporating feedback from current learners who have been through the transition process to improve upon current practice.

Conclusion

Transition is a critical time of change for all involved, but for learners with SEN the experience can have a greater impact. While learners with SEN should be involved with the generic transition activities that are organised by the receiving setting, consideration must be given to their individual needs in order to ensure that the experience is tailored and appropriate. This can be achieved in partnership with the individual's current setting; in consultation with parents and caregivers; and, where possible, in conjunction with the learner. It is vital that this process is smooth as a poor transition can trigger a chain of events that may impact upon future adjustment and academic attainment.

❖ Reflective questions

1. What steps might you consider taking to prepare learners with SEN for transition?

2. How can you ensure the transition process is reflective of individual need?

3. What role do parents and external agencies play in supporting transitions?

Suggested Reading

1. Bunn, H, Davis, D and Speed, E (2017) High School Transition – An Intervention That Empowers Children With Special Educational Needs and Improves School Practice. *Support for Learning*, 32(3): 231–244. [online] Available at: https://doi.org/10.1111/1467-9604.12167 (accessed 13 June 2020).

This article discusses an intervention project undertaken in the East of England to ensure the successful transition of vulnerable pupils in Year 6 to secondary school.

2. Lawson, K and Parker, R (2019) How Do Young People With Special Educational Needs Experience the Transition From School to Further Education? A Review of Literature. *Pastoral Care in Education*, 37(2): 143–61.

The transition of learners with SEN into FE is traditionally low. This article explores the transition experiences of learners with SEN and the impact upon retention.

3. NASEN (2014) *Transition: A Quick Guide to Supporting the Needs of Pupils and Their Families When Moving Between Educational Settings.* [online] Available at: https://nasen.org.uk/uploads/assets/d120f943-7f8b-48c6-bc5b0d2ab448c54d/transition.pdf (accessed 7 May 2020).

This is a quick guide to supporting the needs of learners with SEN and their families when transitioning between educational settings.

References

Bloyce, J and Frederickson, N (2012) Intervening to Improve the Transfer to Secondary School. *Educational Psychology in Practice*, 28(1): 1–18.

Bronfenbrenner, U (1979) *The Ecology of Human Development: Experiments by Nature and Design*. Boston, MA: Harvard University Press.

Bunn, H, Davis, D and Speed, E (2017) High School Transition – An Intervention That Empowers Children With Special Educational Needs and Improves School Practice. *Support for Learning*, 32(3): 231–44. [online] Available at: https://doi.org/10.1111/1467-9604.12167 (accessed 13 June 2020).

Department for Education (2014) *Special Educational Needs and Disability Code of Practice: 0–25 Years*. London: Department for Education.

Department for Education (2018) *Keeping Children Safe in Education*. London: HMSO.

Department for Education (2019) Special Educational Needs: An Analysis and Summary of Data Sources. [online] Available at: https://assets.publishing.service.gov.uk/government/uploads/system/uploads/attachment_data/file/804374/Special_educational_needs_May_19.pdf (accessed 7 June 2020).

Department for Education and Department for Health (2015) Special Educational Needs and Disability Code of Practice: 0 to 25 years. [online] Available at: https://gov.uk/government/uploads/system/uploads/attachment_data/file/398815/SEND_Code_of_Practice_January_2015.pdf (accessed 7 June 2020).

Dockett, S and Perry, B (2016) Supporting Children's Transition to School Age Care. *Australian Educational Research*, 43: 309–26. [online] Available at: https://doi.org/10.1007/s13384-016-0202-y (accessed 7 June 2020).

Doyle, A, McGuckin, C and Shevlin, M (2017) 'Close the Door on Your Way Out': Parent Perspectives on Supported Transition Planning for Young People With Special Educational Needs and Disabilities in Ireland. *Journal of Research in Special Educational Needs*, 17(4): 274–81. [online] Available at: https://doi.org/10.1111/1471-3802.12385 (accessed 7 June 2020).

Estyn (2020) Pupils With Special Educational Needs in Mainstream Schools. A Good Practice Report. [online] Available at: https://estyn.gov.wales/sites/www.estyn.gov.wales/files/documents/Pupils%20with%20special%20educational%20needs%20in%20mainstream%20schools.pdf (accessed 18 February 2020).

Flitcroft, D and Kelly, C (2016) An Appreciative Exploration of How Schools Create a Sense of Belonging to Facilitate the Successful Transition to a New School for Pupils Involved in a Managed Move. *Emotional and Behavioural Difficulties*, 21(3): 301–13. [online] Available at: https://doi.org/10.1080/13632752.2016.1165976 (accessed 7 June 2020).

Hebron, J (2017) The Transition From Primary to Secondary School for Students With Autism Spectrum Conditions. In C Little (ed) *Supporting Social Inclusion for Students with Autism Spectrum Disorders: Insights from Research and Practice* (pp 84–99). London: Routledge.

Hirano, K A, Garbacz, S A, Shanley, L and Rowe, D A (2016) Parent Involvement in Secondary Special Education and Transition: An Exploratory Psychometric Study. *Journal of Child Family Studies*, 25: 3537–53. [online] Available at: https://doi.org/10.1007/s10826-016-0516-4 (accessed 7 June 2020).

Hughes, L A, Banks, P and Terras, M M (2013) Secondary School Transition for Children With Special Educational Needs: A Literature Review. *Support for Learning*, 28(1): 24–34.

Huser, C, Dockett, S and Perry, B (2016) Transition to School: Revisiting the Bridge Metaphor. *European Early Childhood Education Research Journal*, 24(3): 439–49. [online] Available at: http://dx.doi.org/10.1080/1350293X.2015.1102414 (accessed 7 June 2020).

Hutchison, E D (2011) Life Course Theory. In Levesque, R J R (ed) *Encyclopaedia of Adolescence*. New York, NY: Springer.

Kvalsund, R and Bele, I V (2010) Students with Special Educational Needs - Social Inclusion or Marginalisation? Factors of Risk and Resilience in the Transition Between School and Early Adult Life. *Scandinavian Journal of Educational Research*, 54(1): 15–35.

Lave, J and Wenger, E (1990) *Situated Learning: Legitimate Peripheral Participation*. Cambridge, UK: Cambridge University Press.

Lawson, K and Parker, R (2019) How Do Young People With Special Educational Needs Experience the Transition From School to Further Education? A Review of Literature. *Pastoral Care in Education*, 37(2): 143–61.

Morgan, R L, Callow-Heusser, C A, Horrocks E L, Hoffmann, A N and Kupferman, S (2014) Identifying Transition Teacher Competencies Through Literature Review and Surveys of Experts and Practitioners. *Career Development and Transition for Exceptional Individuals*, 37(3): 149–60.

NASEN (2014) Transition: A Quick Guide to Supporting the Needs of Pupils and Their Families When Moving Between Educational Settings. [online] Available at: https://nasen.org.uk/uploads/assets/d120f943-7f8b-48c6-bc5b0d2ab448c54d/transition.pdf (accessed 7 June 2020).

Neal, S, Rice, F, Ng-Knight, T, Riglin, L and Frederickson, N (2016) Exploring the Longitudinal Association Between Interventions to Support the Transition to Secondary School and Child Anxiety. *Journal of Adolescence*, 50: 31–43. [online] Available at: http://dx.doi.org/10.1016/j.adolescence.2016.04.003 (accessed 7 June 2020).

Rice, F, Frederickson, N and Seymour, J (2011) Assessing Pupil Concerns about Transition to Secondary School. *British Journal of Educational Psychology*, 81: 244–263.

Rice, F, Frederickson, N, Shelton, K, McManus, C, Riglin, L and Ng-Knight, T (2015) Identifying Factors That Predict Successful and Difficult Transitions to Secondary School. [online] Available at: https://nuffieldfoundation.org/wp-content/uploads/2019/11/STARS_report.pdf (accessed 7 June 2020).

Sutherland, R, Ching Yee, W, McNess, E and Harris, R (2010) *Supporting Learning in the Transition From Primary to Secondary Schools*. Bristol: University of Bristol. [online] Available at: https://bristol.ac.uk/media-library/sites/cmpo/documents/ transition.pdf (accessed 7 June 2020).

UK Government (2010) *Equality Act*. London: HMSO.

4. LESSONS IN LISTENING I: THE LEARNER'S VOICE

Recap

The previous chapter discussed vulnerable transitions and how they can be supported. It looked at transitions holistically from the view of the learners, the parent or carer and the different stakeholders involved throughout the transition process. This was explored through different theoretical lenses and a variety of strategies were discussed which could be utilised to support vulnerable learners facing transitions. The chapter considered how to empower and build resilience within individuals to ensure they can adapt effectively to new situations. This chapter explores learner perceptions of transition in mainstream settings and how they are supported during the transition process.

Rationale

This chapter explores how learners interpret, navigate and make sense of their experiences during various transition points and across various transition boundaries (Seung Lam and Pollard, 2006). Using learner responses to authenticate the learner voice, a number of different transition points are explored from both a theoretical and practice perspective. Field (2010) argues that transitions need to be viewed both collectively and individually and Dockett (2011) makes the point that transitions in education require changes in the agency and identities of children as they settle themselves in the different educational settings. The role of the learner voice in this chapter is explored by celebrating good practice as well as examining the challenges faced by learners undertaking these transitions. As Dunlop (2003) argues, the first transition experience a learner has may influence the future experiences of transition. Therefore this chapter argues that there is a need to listen to learners about their transition experiences and to use this to inform future practice.

Transition experiences

Learners involved in transition processes were invited to discuss their own experiences of transition. Evidence drawn from their responses will frame the learner perspective as follows.

- Preparation – how the learners were supported before undertaking new transitions.
- Process – how the transition process was facilitated from a learner perspective.
- Outcome – how the learners felt the transition went and how effective it was.

Preparing for transition

Settings have different ways of preparing learners for transition. Nevertheless there is a growing awareness and need for settings to get transitions right. Practitioners, parents and caregivers all play a role in preparing learners for transition and ensuring that the process goes as smoothly as possible. Settings now no longer view transition as a one-off event but as a process that can often start early on in the academic year. Communication between settings and home is actively encouraged and learners are given many opportunities to visit their new or next setting. Sometimes parents and caregivers are invited to accompany their children on visits and are then able to talk about the new setting with their children afterwards. The following responses articulate how learners were prepared for transitions across different settings.

FIRST IMPRESSIONS

Children in Foundation Phase (FP) settings recalled having visited the settings with their parents or caregivers in the summer before starting in September, and then again for an afternoon on their own. They recalled what they remembered about these visits.

- *I had lots of little cars and I played with the bikes. We could play with anything we wanted. I played with the dolls' house* (L1, Reception 1).
- *Mummy said it would be fun and there would be toys* (L2, Reception 1).
- *There were balloons because it was an exciting day. There were lots of things out to play with and I liked the teddies* (L3, Reception 1).
- *I played with someone and then I said you are my best friend* (L4, Reception 1).
- *Me, mummy and daddy were in the car and we talked about starting school. I said to my mummy it's scary. I came in with my mummy and daddy and then I came in on my own* (L1, Reception 2).

These younger learners seem to remember physical resources such as the toys they played with rather than the adults they met. This resonates with findings from Cole and Loftus (1987) who stated that for young children memories are triggered by external cues.

In some places practitioners visited the children at home before they came to the setting.

- *The teachers came to my house and I showed them my toys. Then I visited Nursery with my mammy* (L2, Reception 2).

This resonates with Bronfenbrenner's ecological systems theory (1979) where in the mesosystem the child is influenced not only by the environment but also by relationships between themselves and their families.

NEW EXPERIENCES

Children in Years 1 and 2 experienced *'move up days'* where they spent part of the day or the full day in their new class and recalled how they felt.

- *I was shy, excited and I was scared before I went to my new class but when I got there I was not scared as I went with my friend* (L1, Year 2).
- *I was scared but happy to meet new teachers and it was really fun because they had lots of toys* (L2, Year 2).
- *I remember my new teacher. They let us sit anywhere and they let you pick a partner to sit by* (L3, Year 2).
- *I was excited and scared and anxious* (L4, Year 1).
- *I was excited but when we got back after the summer hols it had changed so that was a bit weird* (L5, Year 2).

Learners in Key Stage 2 (KS2) were asked to recall if they felt prepared for transition to a new class. The responses were mixed, with some feeling they had been adequately prepared, whereas others felt that not enough was done to prepare them.

- *Yes, because I was with my teacher who taught me in Year 2 and my friend* (L1, KS2).
- *Yes, because I was moving up with the same children* (L2, KS2).
- *No, because my teacher didn't give me much information about moving up to a new class* (L3, KS2).
- *Not really, because I joined a late time in the school and felt like I was thrown in without much support* (L4, KS2).
- *Yes, because we had an assembly on moving up day so the headteacher was telling us about it* (L5, KS2).

The responses from these learners resonate with the findings from Niesel and Griebel (2007) who contest that transitions involve feelings of insecurity, nervousness and anxiety but also anticipation and pride. The children who felt more prepared seemed to find security in the familiar with a teacher who had taught them previously, or with the children they already knew. Vygotsky (1978) writes of the more knowledgeable other, and here the learners may have viewed the teachers and the headteacher as those more knowledgeable others and thus felt more secure in the transition process. Ecclestone et al (2006) discuss the relationship between structure and agency throughout the processes and outcomes of transitions. This reinforces the need for learners to feel empowered and have ownership throughout the transitions they are experiencing from the onset.

As can be seen from the interviews with learners from a range of settings, what was important to them in feeling prepared varied. The youngest learners linked feelings of being scared, nervous and excited when visiting settings for the first time. For some of the older learners there were fewer feelings of being scared as they were able to relate their transition experiences to being with friends and the adults who would be with them. In contrast, those children who did not feel prepared seemed to feel that there was a lack of information, especially for those who had started later in the year and had missed the traditional transition activities. This links to Wenger's (1998) community of practice theory where individuals need a sense of community around where and how they belong. The learner who started late in the term did not have this sense of community as reflected in their response of feeling *'thrown in without much support'* (L4, KS2).

TRANSITION EXPERIENCES FOR OLDER LEARNERS

As learners matured, preparation for transition into secondary settings focused more on change-over days and open evenings where they visited their new setting with their parents. These included days where learners were given opportunities to experience different curriculum subjects to those studied at primary school.

- *Different types of days such as PE and other subjects* (L1, secondary school 2).
- *The head of Year 7 came to talk to us in Year 6 and asked us about our feelings* (L2, secondary school 2).
- *There were open evenings where there was an opportunity to meet the teachers and talk to them* (L3, secondary school 2).

For students embarking upon further study in colleges and sixth form settings there were a range of different approaches taken in preparation for transition, such as open days, tours of the new settings and icebreaker activities.

- *Yeah, I went to an open day before* (L1, sixth form).
- *You got to know everyone, we met the teachers and I had a tour of the school* (L2, sixth form).
- *Got to know each other, we did icebreaker tasks and some group tasks where we had to work together* (L3, sixth form).
- *Went on open days where you would get to know everyone* (L1, FE college 1).
- *We did a treasure hunt round college to get to know the buildings and each other. It was much bigger than school* (L2, FE college 1).

Learners recalled still feeling scared about transition into their new settings but recognised the importance of building relationships with others experiencing the same transitions. They recalled specific events such as treasure hunts, group activities and icebreaker activities. This resonates with Bronfenbrenner's ecological systems theory (1979) where in the microsystem the learner is influenced not only by the environment but also by relationships.

The transition process

Next learners were asked to think about the actual transition process and what sort of activities they had done to facilitate this. The actual process of transition can be visualised as a series of different bridges that the learners need to cross (see Galton et al, 1999). For the learners the social and emotional aspects of transition held the most importance (Galton and McLellan, 2018). Here settings recognised that transition was not a one-off event but needed to be a series of events as shown by the learner responses below.

- *We played in the new class, and I painted butterflies. We will have a new yard to play on and we have visited it a few times* (L1, Reception 2).
- *We have been over to the big building lots to see our new class* (L2, Reception 2).
- *I played with new people. We went out in the big yard too* (L3, Reception 2).
- *I went straight to the role-play the first time I visited and then the next time I went to the block-play outside and I went to the mud kitchen* (L1, Year 2).
- *There were animals but they weren't alive and that was different* (L2, Year 2).

Some learners discussed the difference between the class they were in now and the new class they would be going in to.

- *You have to do challenges, six of them in the week and then you get a treat like doing show and tell* (L1, Year 2).
- *Yes, it will be harder and it was harder every time. Reception was easier than Year 1, which was harder; in Year 1 you got to play a little bit. We played more in Reception, but in Year 1 we only played a little bit* (L2, Year 2).
- *In Year 2 you have more jobs to do. We have to go upstairs [Key Stage 2 class was upstairs]. We won't get much choice anymore; it will be more work; there will be different people* (L3, Year 2).
- *In Year 3 we won't be able to go on the bikes and things as we won't get play time when we first go in* (L6, Year 2).

In these responses, learners recalled some of their worries about moving into their new classes and the activities they had undertaken. There seemed to be concerns raised by learners moving from Year 2 into Year 3. Perhaps this is to be expected, as these children were moving not only into a new class but into a new stage of their education (Key Stage 1 to Key Stage 2 in England and from FP to Key Stage 2 in Wales). There were apprehensions over more formal lessons and higher expectations than in their previous stage of education. This resonates with Fisher's (2009) research that formal education can constrain some of the more creative and free thinking evident in younger learners. However, this is an issue that has been recognised by the Welsh Government (WG) who argue for:

ensuring there is awareness and understanding of the nature and requirements of both the Foundation Phase approach and the Key Stage 2 curriculum amongst practitioners and teachers in both learning phases.

(Welsh Government, 2010, p iii)

This supports the work of Sanders et al (2005) who state that in order to alleviate children's concerns over a new classroom or learning environment, then conditions in the new environment should be similar with lots of communication taking place throughout the transition process. Other concerns raised were as follows:

- *There are tables and two people on one table and we have five to a table now. There is lots of choice. It will also be way hotter than downstairs. You can't open the door on to the yard, but you can open the windows though* (L4, Year 2).
- *The class is smaller and we only have one teacher where normally we have three* (L5, Year 2).

Some children identified an issue with the fact they could no longer open the door onto the playground, although they were reassured by being able to open a window. Another concern was raised over the fact there would be fewer adults to support them as learners in Key Stage 2 than they were used to in the Foundation Phase. As Tobbell and O'Donnell (2013) found in their research, students bring understandings and ideas with them from their former classrooms but these understandings may not be the same in the new environment. The settings visited were careful to ensure that children moving within and between key stages had many opportunities to get to know their new environment and new practitioners so any misunderstandings could be sorted out through open days and moving on days.

One learner found the positives in transitioning into a new key stage by stating that:

- *We get to bring our own pencil cases into Year 3. You get a pen if you do good handwriting too in Year 3* (L3, Year 2).

Here there was the excitement of being able to use a pen instead of a pencil and being able to have their own pencil case too. The learners seemed to feel more grown up and empowered in using a pen rather than a pencil.

Learners moving within Key Stage 2 recalled what had happened during their previous transitions.

- *We drew inside a head thing that represented you and what you like and dislike* (L1, KS2).
- *We chose the roles ready for Year 6 such as Reception helper and sorting out the laptop during assembly time* (L2, KS2).
- *We wrote our dreams in a time capsule which we will bury and dig up at the end of next year* (L3, KS2).
- *Because our new teacher didn't know us very well and she got to know us by seeing what our favourite food and drink was, and what country we were born in* (L4, KS2).

These learners seemed to have a more positive outlook on transition into their new class. There was anecdotal evidence of how the new practitioners helped them to settle and got to know them a little better. Again, this links to the microsystem in Bronfenbrenner's ecological systems model (1979) which recognises that the child does not exist in isolation but is influenced by the environment and relationships. The teacher had started to build a relationship with the children and assigned 'job roles' for the coming year. This gives the children a focus and a sense of purpose linking to Maslow (1943) who put a sense of belonging before cognitive needs.

Learners within Year 7 of Key Stage 3 recalled their first days in their new settings.

- *The school felt huge* (L1, secondary school 2).
- *I felt very small* (L2, secondary school 2).

- *I was excited to make new friends but worried about being late for lessons because I didn't know where to go* (L3, secondary school 2).
- *For the first two days we got to know the teachers* (L4, secondary school 2).

The fears raised here are similar to those from the learners moving from Year 2 into Key Stage 2 in primary settings. There was a concern over moving to a larger setting and there being different expectations from previous settings. With reference to Galton et al's (1999) concept of transition as a series of different bridges, the experiences of these learners strongly resonate with the self-management bridge. Here learners need time to get used to more complex arrangements such as bigger settings and to being more organised. The fears over being late and getting lost resonate with the research of Jindal-Snape and Miller (2008) who stated that children were concerned over getting lost in the first weeks of starting at secondary school.

The next set of questions asked learners in post-16 settings to reflect upon their experiences of transition.

CHANGING EXPERIENCES OF TRANSITION

As learners mature and leave compulsory education, there seems to be a more relaxed approach to the overall transition process.

- *We had icebreaker activities in our first week. We went round in a circle and introduced ourselves. We asked each other questions and we feedback but it was really relaxed* (L1, sixth form).
- *We got to know each other, we did icebreaker tasks, some true or false things to get to know the group. You say three things, one is true, the rest are false, and you have to guess which is which. We did this in the first week over two days* (L2, sixth form).
- *We had two days of induction. We did get-to-know-you tasks and we had a homework task where we had to write about what we expected to get from the course and why we wanted to do it. Then the next day we read this out so we got to know each other. We also went on tours of the college in those two days of induction. We had a talk on health and safety; we had a talk from the library staff* (L1, FE college 3).

Here learners felt that they were viewed as young adults and there was an emphasis on the learner voice and what they wanted from their chosen course. Time was spent by practitioners getting to know their new students within a relaxed atmosphere. Hutchison (2011) discussed the importance of the learner voice and how this could support effective transitions. This was evident in the responses given here as the learners all spoke of having time to familiarise themselves with the new settings and getting to know each other. This also resonates with the work of Trotter (2004) and Schoon and Bynner (2003) who identified that activities that promoted students getting to know each other during induction led to a more positive transition experience.

The transition outcome

In all settings visited the learners were asked to consider whether they felt transitions had been handled well and what they would do differently if anything. The first responses focus on what they felt had or had not gone well during this year's transition.

- *Last year and this year we didn't get much advice about moving up and the 'drawing in the head' [a transition activity] doesn't stop you feeling anxious* (L1, KS2).
- *We only had the word from our current teacher that we were staying as a mixed class and I don't feel like we have much information about our new class* (L2, KS2).
- *Because next year is a mixed Year 5/6, the current Year 4's who will be Year 5's next year didn't get to get involved as much because the focus was about the new Year 6* (L3, KS2).

These Key Stage 2 learners felt that they had been at a disadvantage being in a mixed-age class. Here the emphasis had seemed to be more on those learners going into Year 6 and not those going into Year 5, with some children feeling they did not get *'much advice'* or *'information'*. Margetts (2002) discussed the importance of continuity between settings in relationships and learning experiences. Here the Year 4 children felt their voice and needs had been lost, and had feelings of not being as important as the Year 5 children going into Year 6. Harper (2005) notes that learners can feel a loss of voice, control and uniqueness during the transition process and the learners' responses seem to echo this.

Learners in secondary schools were also asked their opinion on how they felt the transition process had gone and if more could have been done to facilitate the transition process.

- *The transition days and open evenings were very good because we could see where everything was* (L1, secondary school 2).
- *There was a lot of information in the transition days* (L2, secondary school 2).
- *It would have been useful to know more about the school's systems. If we were late for lessons then we didn't know there were behaviour steps in place* (L3, secondary school 2).

Again, the responses resonate with Tobbell and O'Donnell's (2013) research that students bring understanding and ideas with them from their former classrooms but that this understanding may not be the same in the new environment. Here the learners felt at a disadvantage in being penalised for being late and they felt this was something that should have been explained during transition. Clear communication is required from the practitioners to the learners to explain the expectations of the new setting, and how this may differ from previous settings.

For learners moving into sixth forms and college settings the following responses were noted.

- *You have to grow up really fast as they expect you to be very independent here* (L2, sixth form).
- *Well it is a step up from level 3 but it seemed a natural step. I was working in setting for seven years so for me it was a lot different so I wasn't as prepared as someone who came from a level*

3 already in college. I think that has shown in some of the work on this course. However, the transition was still really smooth (L1, FE college 1).

- *After the initial transition we still felt we could go and speak to people. We are a really tight group too. We have been lucky to have [our personal tutor] too, she has always been there for all of us* (L1, FE college 2).
- *Yeah, school left us to just get on with it, here they were more supportive, here you can ask the tutors and they help* (L3, FE college 2).

One of the surprising things to come out of these responses is the fact that learners in FE colleges seemed to feel more supported than in school. Learners entering FE felt they had sufficient information about transition and that they had been supported well. They talked of continual support via their personal tutor and felt there were people able to support them after initial transitions or induction. Learners in the sixth form settings did not seem to have the same continuity of care after transition, stating that they *'had to grow up very fast'*. This seems to resonate with one of the learners in FE who compared her transition experience at college to school and felt the college was more supportive.

SUGGESTIONS FOR IMPROVEMENT IN THE TRANSITION PROCESS

The next question focused on what the learners would do differently if they were in charge of transition.

- *I would do similar activities but for the teachers to get involved too so we can learn about them and get to know them as well. We wasted time sorting out stuff with the other classes so next time moving-up day should only be about your class [the school had double-entry classes for each year group]* (L1, KS2).
- *Our current teacher should take you up to your new class and discuss the activities: this would make me feel more relaxed* (L2, KS2).
- *Have a week in your new class so you get used to it more as one day is not enough* (L3, KS2).
- *I would have more time for us to get to know the layout as I still get lost* (L2, sixth form).
- *I would have more time for us to get to know each other before we started lessons* (L3, FE college 2).

What is apparent from these responses is that learners felt they needed more time to get used to their new settings; they wanted more time in their new classroom instead of just one day. They also felt that the transition day should be about the practitioner getting to know them as well as them getting to know the teacher. This supports Vygotsky's sociocultural theory (1978) of every function appearing twice in the child's cultural development, first between people and then inside the child. If the practitioner is able to talk to the learner and build a rapport then the student can internalise this and feel more relaxed about being with the new practitioner in September.

The older students wanted more time to get to know the layout of their new settings, as did some students in FE settings. Some also felt that they wanted more time to get to know fellow students.

This resonates with the work of Harper (2016) who argues for settings to allow time for learners to become familiar with the new setting's grounds and key areas and to spend time in the new environment getting to know the practitioners and other learners.

Findings by O'Toole et al (2014) indicated that adults might have an expectation of increased levels of independence for older learners transitioning into new settings. However, in contrast, the learner responses seem to imply that they did not meet this expectation in independence, still needing reassurance and guidance from the adults.

OPPORTUNITIES FOR FEEDBACK

Learners were asked if they were given the opportunities to feedback on the transitions they had experienced.

- *Yes, the headteacher asked how it was* (L1, KS2).
- *My class teacher asked me how it went* (L2, KS2).
- *We were asked about if we enjoyed the new school. The health and well-being teacher has also asked us if everything was fine* (L1, secondary school 2).
- *We did through our tutorial sessions so that was verbal feedback. We also did feedback online too via a questionnaire. We have course reps too but they have not had to feedback on transition* (L3, FE college 1).

The headteacher and the class teacher had asked learners in Key Stage 2 for their feedback but there was no formal written evidence of how they felt about transition. In the FE setting there was more formal recorded information via a questionnaire but there was no evidence of any feedback to the learners from this. In contrast in a different FE setting, there had been the opportunity for a focus group to meet with the college 'quality department' and for learners to complete learner surveys, learner profiles and feedback to course representatives.

- *We did do a focus group with 'quality' here at the college, about the course and transition. Feedback went to the course leader and she has fed back some of it as it is important we know we are being listened to* (L1, FE college 2).
- *Yeah, we have done a learner-voice survey. We also get opportunities to feedback as a group. We have course reps that also feedback to the module leaders if we have any concerns* (L1, FE college 3).

One FE setting had asked learners to fill in an online questionnaire and one setting had asked students to complete an individual learning profile, with the opportunity to say what had gone well and what they would change.

- *We had to do our first ILP [individual learning profile] about transition. We had to say if it went well or if I would change it. I said we needed more activities in the first few days to settle us in* (L2, FE college 2).

These activities allow students to have a voice in the transition process and show how it can be improved. Trodd (2013, p 164) has discussed how practitioners need to hear children's concerns and allow them to retain *'their agency'*. Although her focus has been early years, this can apply equally to older learners. Asking learners their views on transition supports the rights of young people *'to participate in decisions affecting their lives and communicate their own views'* (Einarsdóttir, 2007, p 75). By giving the learners a voice they were able to feel empowered and that their opinions mattered. Research has shown that learners' concerns around transition are not always the same as adult concerns around transition (Fisher, 2009) and therefore it is important to give them a voice.

Consideration of the learners' voice throughout this chapter has led to the following recommendations for transitions.

Recommendations

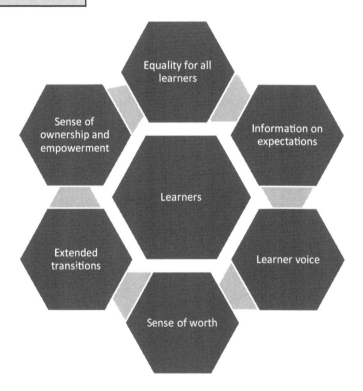

Figure 4.1 Learner recommendations for transitions

- Learners need to have a voice, feel they are being listened to and treated equally and have a sense of worth over the transition process.
- Transitions need to happen over a period of time especially if children are in mixed-aged classes.

- Before moving into a new setting learners could have photos of their new practitioner and classroom environment displayed in their current class. This would allow children to have a sense of ownership over the transition process.
- Settings should send out information on expectations of the new setting to prepare learners before they start, allowing the children to feel more empowered and less fearful of getting things wrong.

Conclusion

This chapter has looked at transition from the perspective of the learner voice. It has discussed how learners are prepared for transition, the transition process and transition outcomes. Learners had experienced a variety of transitions and some seemed to be more positive than others. Settings had undertaken a number of different approaches to transitions from whole days to part days. Here learners had taken part in activities and 'getting to know you' sessions. Feedback on transitions from learners in mixed-age classes indicated that there needed to be a reconceptualisation of the transition process and perhaps a consideration of having separate sessions for different age learners. Students in FE settings seemed happy with the transition process and felt particularly supported throughout the process. All settings visited, from Key Stage 2 onwards, had asked learners for feedback on transition and this ranged from informal discussions to written evidence. This leads to the learners having a sense of agency and empowerment in the transition process.

This chapter has made links to the theories discussed in Chapter 2 and how these theories support the learners in the transition process. The settings have considered the relationship between the learner and the environment, linking to Bronfenbrenner's ecological systems theory (1979). The more knowledgeable other in supporting the learners was evidenced with practitioners talking to the children about transition, linking to Vygotsky's theory (1978). Finally the duration of transitions as not one-off events were demonstrated by some settings. This was achieved through displaying photos of the new classroom and the new practitioners in the summer term before learners returned to their new settings in September. This supports life-course theory and practitioners preparing learners for transition in plenty of time (Hutchison, 2011). This chapter has sought to present the importance of understanding transition from the perspective of the learner and the importance of the learner voice. This can best be summed up by the following learner comments which support the growing awareness by learners and settings alike that transition is no longer a singular event but an ongoing evolving process.

- *I think that transition isn't just when you start, you need support all the way through. When I went to college years ago I started to go off the rails summer time when the work got harder, I was expected to get on with it because transition was done but that was when I still needed some support. Now I think things are taken more seriously with continued support offered. Maybe I know how to look for it better but that continual support is really, really important and is one of the factors that has allowed me to stick at it* (L3, FE college 3).

❖ Reflective questions

1. How does your setting currently prepare learners for transitions?

2. Having read this chapter are there any ways your setting could improve transitions for learners?

3. How do you ensure the learner's voice is supported during and after transitions?

4. On reflection, what is your role in the transition process and can this be improved?

Suggested reading

1. Trodd, L (2013) (ed) *Transitions in the Early Years*. London: SAGE.

Brings together theory and practice with case studies from different perspectives.

2. Dunlop, A and Fabian, H (2007) (eds) *Informing Transitions in the Early Years*. Berkshire: Open University Press.

This book explores transitions from a variety of international perspectives. It is underpinned by research and offers recommendations for practitioners in understanding transitions more fully.

3. Ecclestone, K, Biesta, G and Hughes, M (2010) (eds) *Transitions Through the Lifecourse*. London: Routledge.

This book combines data and theoretical approaches to provide an insight into transitions.

References

Bronfenbrenner, U (1979) *The Ecology of Human Development: Experiments by Nature and Design*. Boston, MA: Harvard University Press.

Cole, C and Loftus, E (1987) The Memory of Children. In Ceci, S, Toglia, M and Ross, D (eds) *Children's Eye-Witness Memory*. New York: Springer-Verlag.

Dockett, S (2011) *Transition to School: Normative or Relative?* Paper presented at the EECERA conference, Geneva.

Dunlop, A W (2003) *Bridging Children's Early Education Transitions Through Teacher Collaboration*. Paper presented at the New Zealand Association for Research in Education and Australian Association for Research in Education Joint Conference, November 29–December 3, Auckland, Australia.

Ecclestone, K, Blackmore, T, Biesta, G, Colley, H and Hughes, M (2006) Lost in Transition: Managing Change and Becoming Through Education and Work. Nottingham: TLRP Seminar Series *Transitions Through the Life Course*, Seminar 12-13 October 2006.

Einarsdóttir, J (2007) Children's Voice on the Transitions from Preschool to Primary School. In Dunlop, F and Fabian, H (eds) *Informing Transitions in the Early Years*. Berkshire: Open University Press.

Field, J (2010) Preface. In Ecclestone, K, Biesta, G and Hughes, M (eds) *Transitions and Learning Through the Life Course*. London: Routledge.

Fisher J (2009) We Used to Play in Foundation, It Was More Funner: Investigating Feelings About Transition From Foundation Stage to Year 1. *Early Years*, 29(2), 131-45. [online] Available at: https://doi.org/10.1080/09575140802672576 (accessed 7 June 2020).

Galton, M, Gray, J and Ruddock, J (1999) *The Impact of School Transitions and Transfers on Pupil Progress and Attainment*. London: HMSO.

Galton, M and McLellan, R (2018) A Transition Odyssey: Pupils' Experiences of Transfer to Secondary School Across Five Decades. *Research Papers in Education*, 33:2, 255-77. [online] Available at: https://doi.org/10.1080/02671522.2017.1302496 (accessed 7 June 2020).

Harper, L J (2005) *Transition Voices: Perspectives, Concerns, and Discontinuities Expressed by Children, Parents and Teachers as Children Transition From a University-affiliated Kindergarten to a Public School First Grade*. Unpublished doctoral dissertation, University of New Hampshire.

Harper, L J (2016) Supporting Young Children's Transitions to School: Recommendations for Families. *Early Childhood Education Journal*, 44: 653-9.

Hutchison, E D (2011) Life Course Theory. In Levesque, R J R (ed) *Encyclopaedia of Adolescence*. New York, NY: Springer.

Jindal-Snape, D and Miller, D (2008) A Challenge of Living? Understanding the Psycho-social Processes of the Child During the Primary–Secondary Transition Through Resilience and Self-esteem Theories. *Education Psychology Review*, 20: 217-36.

Margetts, K (2002) Transition to School - Complexity and Diversity. *European Early Childhood Education Research Journal*, 10(2): 103-14.

Maslow, A H (1943) A Theory of Human Motivation. *Psychological Review*, 50(4): 370-96.

Morris, M, McCrindle, L, Cheung, J, Johnson, R, Pietikainen, A and Smith, R (2010) *Exploring Education Transitions for Pupils Aged 6- 8 in Wales*. [online] Available at: https://gov.wales/sites/default/files/statistics-and-research/2019-08/110314exploringeducationtransitionsforpupilsaged6-8inwalesen.pdf (accessed 7 June 2020).

Niesel, R and Griebel, W (2007) Enhancing the Competence of Transition Systems Through Co-Construction. In Dunlop, A W and Fabian, H (eds) *Informing Transitions in the Early Years*. London: McGraw-Hill Open University Press.

O'Toole, L, Hayes, N and Mhic Mhathúna, M (2014) A Bio-Ecological Perspective on Educational Transition. *Social and Behavioral Sciences*, 140: 121-7. [online] Available at: https://doi.org/10.21427/D7GP4Z (accessed 7 June 2020).

Sanders, D, White, G, Burge, B, Sharp, C, Eames, A, Mceune, R and Grayson, H (2005) *A Study of the Transition From the Foundation Stage to Key Stage 1*. London: National Foundation for Educational Research.

Schoon, I and Bynner, J (2003) Risk and Resilience in the Life Course. Implications for Interventions and Social Policies. *Journal of Youth Studies*, 6(1): 21-31.

Seung Lam, M and Pollard, A (2006) A Conceptual Framework for Understanding Children as Agents in the Transition From Home to Kindergarten. *Early Years*, 26(2): 123-41. [online] Available at: https://doi.org/10.1080/09575140600759906 (accessed 7 June 2020).

Tobbell, J and O'Donnell, V L (2013) Transition to Postgraduate Study: Postgraduate Ecological Systems and Identity. *Cambridge Journal of Education*, 43(1): 123-38. [online] Available at: https://doi.org/10.1080/0305764X.2012.749215 (accessed 7 June 2020).

Trodd, L (2013) *Transitions in the Early Years*. London: SAGE.

Trotter, E (2004) *Enhancing the Early Student Experience*. Paper presented at Conference on Education in a Changing Environment. September 2004, University of Salford.

Vygotsky, L (1978) *Mind in Society. The Development of Higher Psychological Processes*. Cambridge, MA: Harvard University Press.

Wenger, E (1998) *Communities of Practice: Learning, Meaning and Identity*. New York: Cambridge University Press.

5. LESSONS IN LISTENING 2: GIVING VOICE TO THE LEARNER'S SUPPORT SYSTEM

Recap

The previous chapter considered transitions from the perspective of the learner. It explored some of the ways learners were prepared (and prepared themselves) for transition. Learners experience a variety of transitions during their time in education and there was no uniform approach to transition. However some experiences were more positive than others, and different approaches did give a sense of empowerment and agency. Clear links were made to theory and what could be learnt from this perspective in terms of transition. Bronfenbrenner's ecological systems theory (1979) and reference to Vygotsky's more knowledgeable other (1978) were both helpful in terms of recognising how dependent learners are on the approach taken by practitioners during this time. Chapter 4 showed how important learner voice is in ensuring a successful transition. It also evidenced the importance of recognising that transition is not just about the move from one place to another but an ongoing process that needs to be recognised and discussed.

Rationale

While the value of the learner voice is recognised, it is equally important to understand the importance of parent voice during times of transition. Miller (2014) points out that despite few studies exploring parental experiences of transition, it is recognised that their experiences of education can have a direct impact on their children's. It has been argued that parents' memories of school get reactivated when preparing their children for school (Taylor et al, 2004). Parents and caregivers, therefore, play a very important part in successful transitions. As well as providing learners with emotional and physical support – as explained through Bronfenbrenner's ecological systems theory (1979) – the relationship they have with settings and other stakeholders has a significant impact on the learner's academic achievement and general well-being. Therefore the role of parents during this time is extremely important and can be pivotal to the learner's successful transition and ongoing learning experience. According to Sheldon (2009) parents have a number of important functions to fulfil if learners are to have not only a successful transition, but positive academic experience. In line with Maslow's 'hierarchy of needs' (2013), they need to provide safe physical environments, adequate nutrition and positive relationships.

While it is clear that the learner should be at the centre of the transition experience, it is also important to recognise that parents experience it too. As much as they can be considered *'agents of change* they are also subject to changes themselves. This is especially true as children get older and the expectations and relationships parents have with schools, and how they communicate with them, change. Adapting to these new circumstances and ways of working can be challenging and can involve shifts in identity for parents as much as learners (Osborn et al, 2006). This means that there needs to be good collaboration between settings and parents if all involved are to successfully navigate the complex and wide impact of transitioning to new settings (Griebel and Niesel, 2009). Miller (2014) argues the need for a transition framework, within which there need to be programmes which are more inclusive and supportive of parents' views and understandings. He also argues that there is a need within these programmes to give a clear voice to parents' experiences of their child's transitions (Webb et al, 2017).

However more often than not parental involvement in transition is seen as a way to address the setting's agenda (concerning the learners and the school itself), and the role changes and challenges parents face are often overlooked. Frequently it is practitioners who construct the transition, but it is the parents who support the social and developmental tasks taking place. Transition therefore should be a process of co-construction between practitioners, learners and parents/caregivers (Griebel and Niesel, 2002, cited in Griebel and Niesel, 2009).

To get a clearer picture of the experiences and expectations of transitions the following areas were considered:

- preparation – how parents were prepared for transition and how they prepared themselves;
- process – how parents were involved in the transition process;
- outcome – how parents felt about the process.

Transition experiences

Understanding of the role parents/caregivers play in the transition experiences of their children continues to evolve as educational systems pay more attention to the holistic development of children. Knowing that social and emotional aspects of learning provide the foundations for successful achievement and attainment impacts significantly on how educational settings view, among other things, the role of parents during the educational process. Historically, this has not always been the case. Schools had been conceived only as places of academic study and the moral, cultural and religious education of children was the responsibility of their family (Hill and Taylor, 2004). When the Education Act 1944 reformed the way children were educated, it focused mostly on attainment. At 11 children took the 11+ exam and were then placed in one of three different types of school according to the results: grammar schools for the most academic; technical colleges for those who had technical and vocational skills; and secondary modern schools for those who were considered to be neither academic nor practical. The review of this system in the 1960s, and the Plowden Report (1967) that followed, identified key failings and recommended that children should be placed at its centre and, significantly, that parents should be involved. The three-tier system was slowly abandoned with a two-tier system of primary education followed by a transition to secondary taking its place.

More recently, the role of parents in their children's education as a whole, and in the transitions that take place, has been recognised as an extremely important one. The boundaries of roles and responsibilities between school and home have also become much more fluid. In 1995 the World Health Organization first set out the importance of both home and school being responsible for pupils' well-being. Then the connection between pupils' well-being and good partnerships (Roffey, 2012) was connected to their academic success as well.

Good partnerships between settings must have meaningful bi-directional communication to ensure proximal process (Griffore and Phenice, 2016, p 11). If done well, partnerships during the transition process will support the child at what is potentially a very difficult time, as well as being a precursor to ongoing and more meaningful relationships between the parents and the setting (Griebel and Niesel, 2009). With the increased importance given to accountability and demands for children to do well, it behoves practitioners to work in partnership with parents (Hill and Taylor, 2004).

The importance of parental involvement

There is a persistent relationship recognised between parents' attainment in school and that of their child (McNeal Jr, 1999). Taylor et al (2004) suggest that parents' attitudes, values and beliefs about schooling influence their use of transition practices, which, in turn, contribute to children's early outcomes during transition to school. It is also recognised that parents' own experience of education can dictate their attitude to their child's school, which can have both a positive and negative effect on the child (Taylor et al, 2004). This means that parents who either have little or no experience of the educational system, or had a bad experience of school themselves, are likely to have a negative impact on their child's attainment (Sutherland et al, 2010). There is also a connection to socioeconomic background, with research finding that parents with low socioeconomic status (SES) often feel ill-equipped to question teachers or schools and potentially harbour more negative experiences with schools than their more advantaged peers (Lareau, 1996). As such it has been argued that students from lower-SES homes often lack the parental support that enables a successful transition. Parents from low SES homes tend to be less involved in collaborative partnerships with practitioners. It is important, therefore, that settings develop a more inclusive transition process to better take into account the *'stories of parents from socioeconomically disadvantaged and culturally diverse contexts'* (Webb et al, 2017, p 208).

Understanding and listening to the stories of parents is particularly significant when considering how to ensure effective transitions. While transitions for learners often coincide with changes in identity, construction of self and issues to do with self-esteem (Osborn et al, 2006), they also impact on existing relationships. For example, the transition from primary to secondary is a systemic transition (a bigger school, more departmentalisation and tracking, greater emphasis on relative ability) and one that coincides with early adolescence, a time of marked social, biological and psychological development (Anderson et al, 2000). Anderson et al (2000) also point out that systemic transitions affect nearly all students in some way, in terms of either falling attainment, negative attitudes to some subjects and teachers or a decrease in self-efficacy and self-esteem. Not only are learners navigating new environments, they are also having to establish new relationships and develop new ways of learning. This is disruptive and often means that previously learned behaviour patterns need to be adapted to new demands, which can put a strain on existing relationships and achievement (Ding, 2008, p 305). It becomes increasingly important, therefore, that during a time of potential vulnerability, all relationships are considered – including the relationship between parents and the school (Britto, 2012). Positive parental involvement is doubly important because it supports academic achievement and has a powerful influence on positive social and psychological outcomes, especially for primary aged children (Blake Berryhill, 2016).

Preparation for transition

Effective transitions consider and engage with the child's own learner identity (Osborn et al, 2006), what is known about the parents' experiences of education, and their role as primary agents of a learner's socialisation during early childhood (Puccioni, 2015). This is a way of ensuring school readiness for both parents and children. The concepts of school readiness and school transition are very closely linked (Correia and Marques-Pinto, 2016). *'Ready schools'* reach out to families, build relationships between families and the school setting before the first day of school (Hill and Taylor, 2004) and in turn parents prepare their child for the setting. Parental expectations of the child's readiness for school have been defined in terms of what the parent believes their child is capable of academically (Puccioni, 2015) and what skills are needed to attend the setting. For children entering the early years, it is likely that parents will prepare them for school by helping them to acquire new skills and knowledge, taking on the role of the *'more knowledgeable other'* (Vygotsky, 1978). This academic or skills-based preparation for transition seems to grow less common as children transition further along, with priorities for transition from primary to secondary focused on friendship groups, logistics and safety.

- *We spent time going through pictures taken of the new setting, discussed worries eg where the toilets are, my friends staying with me* (Pt, Year 2).
- *Talk about how they are feeling, did they like their new classroom. Discuss and deal with any worries they may have* (Pt, Year 2).

Parental experience and engagement

Bronfenbrenner's ecological systems theory (1979) provides a useful model when considering the wider context of transition and how each individual involved in it is influenced. The reciprocal interactions between environment, objects, symbols and individuals are what create the proximal process (Griffore and Phenice, 2016). This means that the wider context of home life, parental experience and engagement has to be considered as much as direct social interactions and communications between individuals. It is also important to recognise that proximal process is a sequence of events (Bronfenbrenner and Morris, 2006), which ties in with the recognition, as identified in Chapter 4, that transition happens on a continuum and is often much longer and much more complex than has been traditionally envisioned.

Parental involvement, when it is consistent and meaningful, can affect the child's progress before and after the transition, especially when it is done well, and the setting seeks to provide a basis for long-term involvement with the school. Where this occurs, there is the added benefit of increasing the likelihood the child will achieve more, get higher grades and behave better (Mizelle, 2005). This is seen in the type of conversations parents explained that they had had with their children preparing them for expectations of school that mirrored their own.

- *Lots of discussion about what to expect will happen. Reading books about new schools* (Pt, Year 2).
- *Positive discussions. Involving them in purchasing uniform* (Pt, Year 2).
- *We spoke to Ruby and shared our own experiences of high school. We explained it would open up opportunities* (Pt, secondary school 2).

Developing positive relationships with settings

Positive relationships between the school and parents/caregivers often motivate children (Hoover-Dempsey et al, 2005). However, how parents are involved with their child's school during the transition process varies widely according to setting and location. In general, their involvement is generally seen in terms of volunteering in the school, communicating with the staff, supporting academic activities and attending parent–teacher conferences (Hill and Taylor, 2004).

The data gathered shows that a parent's own experiences as a practitioner can have a positive effect on preparing a child for education.

- *I am a Nursery/Reception teacher, so I had worked with Noah on nursery rhymes, numbers, colours, etc. I had prepared him for Nursery by taking him to play groups* (Pt, Reception 1).

Where parents also have a lot of contact with multi-agency workers for a variety of reasons, their involvement with transition becomes pivotal, for example in the case of children with specific additional needs.

- *Isobel, because of her health and developmental issues, has had contact with various agencies. Prior to starting school Isobel had had portage, attended a children's centre for Nursery activities and attended Flying Start Nursery. All the above helped her easy transition into formal Nursery* (Pt, Reception 1).

During transition

Evidence collected suggests that most parental involvement during transitions follows the norm. Parents fit into a supporting, rather than partnership, role. In most instances, as learners move through educational settings, parents increasingly play a passive role. This is despite the fact that it is the home environment that has the most impact on the child and their education choices (Van Rens et al, 2018).

- *We attended open nights at the school in Year 5 and Year 6. We discussed moving up and the changes as a family* (Pt, secondary school 2).
- *The primary school arranged for transitions days* (Pt, secondary school 2).
- *Both the schools did an excellent job of managing Elin's expectations and familiarisation* (Pt, secondary school 2).

As well as attending some transition days, parents also provided emotional support at home in terms of discussions and expectations.

- *We spoke a lot about it* (Pt, Reception 2).
- *As a family, we would talk of what school will be like and would drive past and tell Billie this is where she would be going. Billie was fully involved when buying uniforms and bags etc* (Pt, Reception 1).

PAST EXPERIENCES OF TRANSITIONS

Evidence from data collected suggests that previous experience of parents and learners' siblings is also important in terms of preparing the learner for transition.

- *My son had already been through transition previously. Was able to tell her all about it* (Pt, Year 2).
- *She has seen older siblings transition* (Pt, Year 2).
- *James is familiar with the school and the site due to older siblings* (Pt, Reception 2).

Utilising this relationship more, recognising the skills that parents bring to the partnership, is important because of the *'persistent relationship'* between a parent's attainment and that of their child (McNeal Jr, 1999, p 118). This affirms the need for bi-directional, reciprocal communication between settings and parents.

VALUE ADDED: WHAT PARENTS BRING

Building positive relationships with parents before, during and after transition is a powerful tool in terms of supporting children's learning and achievement. Positive parental interactions with the school are one of the most widely recognised factors impacting on a child's learning and development (Blake Berryhill, 2016). For example, in terms of the transition from primary to secondary – considered one of the most difficult in pupils' educational experience (Zeedyk et al, 2003) – parental involvement can prevent the 'dip' in attainment at the start of secondary school (Greenhough, 2007).

Parents can provide valuable extra activities to support successful transitions. Some parents interviewed identified a wider approach to transition beyond the confines of the school setting.

- *[We] encouraged her to participate with joint activities with other schools. We also enrolled her in a local netball team with the aim of enabling her to get to know children who would be in her year* (Pt, secondary school 2).

- *I arranged for my daughter to meet pupils who went to the school, to make friends and ask questions about the new school* (Pt, secondary school 2).

HOW TO INVOLVE PARENTS

Involving parents with the transition process needs to be carefully considered and thorough, with a clear recognition that *'parent-school relationships do not occur in insolation, but in community and cultural contexts'* (Hill and Taylor, 2004, p 162). Involvement can be through direct participation, academic encouragement and shared expectations for attainment (Chen and Gregory, 2009). What is recognised is that if parents remain a constant support for their child, monitor their activities and intervene positively, then the child is likely to have a smooth transition (Hanewald, 2013). Where the school and the parents are not in line with each other, parental support is likely to be less effective (McGee et al, 2004).

PARENTAL TRANSITIONS

One important aspect to realise is that as children go through key transitions, parents are also experiencing a transition of their own. They are having to cope with change and fear of the unknown; as true in the transition from early years to primary, as primary to secondary. Research by Correia and Marques-Pinto (2016) identified parents recognising anxiety about creating new relationships with teachers and their children's friends. There is a change in expectations of the relationship as learners progress through the educational system. This is particularly marked when learners transition from primary to secondary school. With secondary settings, parents no longer enjoy the reasonably ready access they had to their child's teacher in primary and have to create new relationships with a number of different teachers (Coffey, 2013). It can often bring about a change in parenting roles with a focus on facilitating their child's growing independence, supported by reconfiguring of communication channels with the setting. Unlike primary schools, children now deliver information to the parent, rather than it coming directly from the school (Bagnall et al, 2019).

The transition from primary to secondary school is often seen as a *'rite of passage'* and can be associated with *'strong feelings of loss'* (Bagnall et al, 2019, p 7) and a sense *'that their child was growing up'* (p 8). There is similar anxiety associated with the move from preschool to primary, which has been regarded by school teachers as a factor that generates stress in the child. If it is recognised that parents shape and develop their children's prosocial and antisocial behaviours, in accordance with Bronfenbrenner's ecological systems model (1979), then their anxiety can influence the child's behaviour. This can lead to parents repressing emotions which leaves both them and their children feeling alone in their apprehension towards transition (Bagnall et al, 2019).

However, what becomes clear is that the further children progress through education, the less involvement parents have with the school. Assumptions to do with maturity and independence of learning the further a child goes into their educational experience mean that opportunities for relationship development between parents and schools are at best underdeveloped and at worst ignored (Tobbell and O'Donnell, 2013).

ALL CHANGE!

It is also worth noting that transition is often a much longer process than sometimes believed – with children at secondary school often still considered to be transitioning well into Year 8 (Osborn et al, 2006). Therefore the importance of ongoing relationships with parents beyond what is traditionally considered the transition period cannot be overestimated.

Recommendations

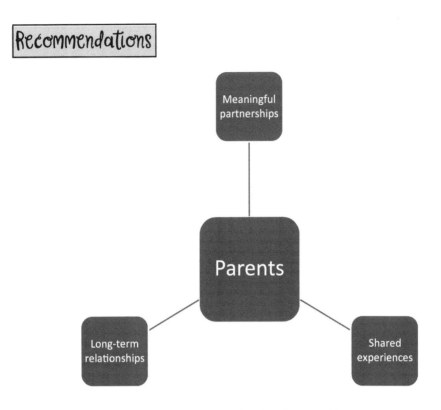

Figure 5.1 Key features for preparing parents for effective transitions

Analysing responses from parents, and with support from the literature, has highlighted three key features that need to be considered when planning for effective transitions.

- Partnerships between schools and parents need to be meaningful and based on bi-directional, well-informed communication.
- Sharing parents' own experiences of transition and education in a safe forum helps schools recognise the support parents might need if they are going to play an effective role in their child's transition process.
- Effective communication and building relationships with parents will lead to long-term relationships between home and school which will have a positive impact on the child's motivation to learn and achieve.

Conclusion

While much emphasis is placed, rightly, on the learner's experiences of transition, the experiences of parents and their social and emotional response to their child's transition are often overlooked. It is apparent that transitions can be extremely difficult and emotional for both parent and learner for a number of reasons. For both, there are new routines to follow, new environments to navigate and new relationships to be created and developed. For some parents this can be challenging because of their own experiences in education and their own aptitudes and dispositions towards school. However, there is little evidence to suggest that much has been done to explore what support and what needs parents might have in terms of their own socio-emotional well-being during their children's transitions. This makes it clear that more research needs to be done not just in terms of what advantages and skills parents can provide during the transition period, but what they need in order to be able to offer that support. If schools better understand the types of adjustments parents have to make during these times and what they can do to support the parents, it is possible to argue that transitions will become more effective for all those involved. To be able to achieve this there needs to be more information available and effective communication between parents and schools, which is bi-directional and meaningful, rather that institutionalised. This will mean that parents can be truly agentic in their child's transitional process and transitions can be effective.

❖ Reflective questions

1. How can schools encourage further parental involvement where there are issues of poor prior experience with parents?

2. How do settings ensure the stories of parents are heard?

3. What support is needed to ensure parents are not stressed by the changes as their child transitions?

Suggested reading

Miller, K (2014) From Past to Present: How Memories of School Shape Parental Views of Children's Schooling. *International Journal of Early Years Education*, 23(2): 153–71. [online] Available at: https://doi.org/10.1080/09669760.2014.992869 (accessed 13 June 2020).

This journal article brings together experiences from a sample of 24 parents from lower income backgrounds who discuss how they prepare their child for kindergarten and their memories of school. It examines the link between their recollections and their thoughts and behaviours as they prepare their children.

Webb, G, Knight, B and Busch, G (2017) Children's Transition to School: 'So What About Parents'? or 'So, What About the Parents'? *International Journal of Early Years Education*, 25(2): 204–17. [online] Available at: https://doi.org/10.1080/09669760.2017.1301808 (accessed 13 June 2020).

This journal article uses the bioecological model to consider childhood transitions as social, political and highly contextualised experiences. It argues that parents need support during this period and that schools need to provide suitable support and time for parents to share their own experiences of transitions to school.

Cheung, C S and Pomerantz, E M (2012) Why Does Parents' Involvement Enhance Children's Achievement? The Role of Parent-orientated Motivation. *Journal of Educational Psychology*, 104(3): 820–32. [online] Available at: https://doi.org/10.1037/a0027183 (accessed 13 June 2020).

This journal article looks at the impact parents' involvement has on their child's attainment and achievement in school. The research considered the role parents played in their child's motivation to learn and achieve and how in enhanced self-regulated learning.

References

Anderson, L W, Jacobs, J, Schramm, S and Splittgerber, F (2000) School Transitions: Beginning of the End or a New Beginning? *International Journal of Educational Research*, 33(4): 325–39. [online] Available at: https://doi.org/10.1016/S0883-0355(00)00020-3 (accessed 7 June 2020).

Bagnall, C, Skipper, Y and Fox, C (2019) 'You're in This World Now': Students', teachers', and Parents' Experiences of School Transition and How They Feel It Can Be Improved. *British Journal of Educational Psychology*, 90(1): 206–26. [online] Available at: https://doi.org/10.1111/bjep.12273 (accessed 7 June 2020).

Blake Berryhill, M (2016) Co-Parenting and Parental School Involvement. *Child Youth Care Forum*, 46: 261–83. [online] Available at: https://doi.org/10.1007/s10566-016-9384-8 (accessed 7 June 2020).

Britto, P (2012) *School Readiness and Transition*. New York: UNICEF.

Bronfenbrenner, U (1979) *The Ecology of Human Development: Experiments by Nature and Design*. Boston, MA: Harvard University Press.

Bronfenbrenner, U and Morris, P A (2006) The Biological Model of Human Development. In Damon, W and Lerner R M (eds) *Handbook of Child Psychology, Vol 1: Theoretical Models of Human Development*. New York: John Wiley and Sons, Inc.

Chen, W and Gregory, A (2009) Parental Involvement as a Protective Factor During the Transition to High School. *The Journal of Educational Research*, 103(1): 53–62. [online] Available at: https://doi.org/10.1080/00220670903231250 (accessed 7 June 2020).

Coffey, A (2013) Relationships: The Key to Successful Transition From Primary to Secondary School? *Improving Schools*, 16(3): 261–71. [online] Available at: https://doi.org/10.1177/1365480213505181 (accessed 7 June 2020).

Correia, K and Marques-Pinto, A (2016) Adaptation in the Transition to School: Perspectives of Parents, Preschool and Primary School Teachers. *Educational Research*, 58(3): 247-64. [online] Available at: https://doi.org/10.1080/00131881.2016.1200255 (accessed 7 June 2020).

Ding, C S (2008) Variations in Academic Performance Trajectories During High School Transition: Exploring Change Profiles via Multidimensional Scaling Growth Profile Analysis. *Educational Research and Evaluation*, 14(4): 305-19. [online] Available at: https://doi.org/10.1080/13803610802249357 (accessed 7 June 2020).

Education Act (1944). [online] Available at: http://educationengland.org.uk/documents/acts/1944-education-act.html (accessed 25 May 2020).

Greenhough, P (2007) *What Effect Does Involving Parents in Knowledge Exchange Activities During Transfer From Key Stage 2 to Key Stage 3 Have on Children's Attainment and Learning Dispositions?* Paper presented at the British Educational Research Association Annual Conference, Institute of Education, 5-8 September, London, UK.

Griebel, W and Niesel, R (2009) A Developmental Psychology Perspective in Germany: Co-Construction of Transitions Between Family and Education System By the Child, Parents and Pedagogues. *Early Years: An International Research Journal*, 29: 59-68. [online] Available at: https://doi.org/10.1080/09575140802652230 (accessed 25 May 2020).

Griffore, R and Phenice, L (2016) Proximal Processes and Causality in Human Development. *European Journal of Educational Development Psychology*, 4(1): 10-16.

Hanewald, R (2013) Transition Between Primary and Secondary School: Why It Is Important and How It Can Be Supported. *Australian Journal of Teacher Education*, 38(1): 62-74. [online] Available at: https://doi.org/10.14221/ajte.2013v38n1.7 (accessed 7 June 2020).

Hill, N and Taylor, L (2004) Parental School Involvement and Children's Academic Achievement: Pragmatics and Issues. *Current Directions in Psychological Science*, 13: 161-4.

Hoover-Dempsey, K, Walker, M, Sandler, H, Whetsel, D, Green, C, Wilkins, A and Closson, K (2005) Why Do Parents Become Involved? Research Findings and Implications. *The Elementary School Journal*, 106: 105-30.

Lareau, A (1996) Assessing Parent Involvement in Schooling: A Critical Analysis. In Booth, A and Dunn, J F (eds) *Family-School Links: How Do They Affect Educational Outcomes?* Mahwah, NJ: Lawrence Erlbaum Associates, Inc.

Maslow, A (2013) A Theory of Human Motivation. *Psychological Review*, 50: 370-96. [online] Available at: https://doi.org/10.1037/h0054346 (accessed 7 June 2020).

McGee, C, Ward, R, Gibbons, J and Harlow, A (2004) *Transition to Secondary School: A Literature Review*. Hamilton: Waikato Institute for Research in Learning Curriculum School of Education, University of Waikato.

McNeal, R B Jr (1999) Parental Involvement as Social Capital: Differential Effectiveness on Science Achievement, Truancy, and Dropping Out. *Social Forces*, 78: 117-44. [online] Available at: https://doi.org/10.1093/sf/78.1.117 (accessed 7 June 2020).

Miller, K (2014) From Past to Present: How Memories of School Shape Parental Views of Children's Schooling. *International Journal of Early Years Education*, 23: 1-19. [online] Available at: https://doi.org/10.1080/09669760.2014.992869 (accessed 7 June 2020).

Mizelle, N B (2005) Moving Out of Middle School. *Educational Leadership*, 62(7): 56–60.

Osborn, M, McNess, E and Pollard, A (2006) Identity and Transfer: A New Focus for Home-School Knowledge Exchange. *Educational Review*, 58(4): 415–33. [online] Available at: https://doi.org/10.1080/00131910600971867 (accessed 7 June 2020).

Plowden Report (1967) *Children and Their Primary Schools*. London: HMO.

Puccioni, J (2015) Parents' Conceptions of School Readiness, Transition Practices and Children's Academic Achievement Trajectories. *The Journal of Educational Research*, 108: 130–47. [online] Available at: https://doi.org/10.1080/00220671.2013.850399 (accessed 7 June 2020).

Roffey, S (2012) Developing Positive Relationships in Schools. In Roffey, S (ed) *Positive Relationships: Evidence Based Practice Across the World*. London: Springer.

Sheldon, S B (2009) *School, Family and Community Partnerships: Your Handbook for Action* (third edition). USA: Corwin Press.

Sutherland, R, Ching Yee, W, McNess, E and Harris, R (2010) *Supporting Learning in the Transition From Primary to Secondary Schools*. Bristol: University of Bristol. [online] Available at: https://bristol.ac.uk/media-library/sites/cmpo/documents/transition.pdf (accessed 7 June 2020).

Taylor, L C, Clayton, J D and Rowley, S J (2004) Academic Socialization: Understanding Parental Influences on Children's School-related Development in the Early Years. *Review of General Psychology*, 8(3): 163–78. [online] Available at: https://doi.org/10.1037/1089-2680.8.3.163 (accessed 7 June 2020).

Tobbell, J and O'Donnell, V L (2013) Transition to Postgraduate Study: Postgraduate Ecological Systems and Identity. *Cambridge Journal of Education*, 43(1): 123–38. [online] Available at: https://doi.org/10.1080/0305764X.2012.749215 (accessed 7 June 2020).

Van Rens, M, Haelermans, C, Groot, W and Maassen van den Brink, H (2018) Facilitating a Successful Transition to Secondary School: (How) Does It Work? A Systematic Literature Review. *Adolescent Research Review*, 3: 43–56. [online] Available at: https://link.springer.com/article/10.1007/s40894-017-0063-2 (accessed 7 June 2020).

Vygotsky, L (1978) *Mind in Society. The Development of Higher Psychological Processes*. Cambridge, MA: Harvard University Press.

Webb, G, Knight, B and Busch, G (2017) Children's Transitions to School: 'So What About Parents'? or 'So, What About the Parents'? *International Journal of Early Years Education*, 25(2): 204–17. [online] Available at: https://doi.org/10.1080/09669760.2017.1301808 (accessed 7 June 2020).

Zeedyk, S M, Gallacher, J, Henderson, M, Hope, G, Husband, B and Lindsay, K (2003) Negotiating the Transition from Primary to Secondary School. Perceptions of Pupils, Parents and Teachers. *School Psychology International*, 24: 67–79. [online] Available at: https://doi.org/10.1177/0143034303024001010 (accessed 7 June 2020).

6. PRACTITIONER DISCOURSE: PREPARING FOR AND SUPPORTING TRANSITIONS

Recap

The previous chapter explored the critical role parents/caregivers play in supporting children and young people through transition experiences. It discussed the value of parent voice and how parental experiences of transition can have a direct impact on the transition experiences of their children, not only from an emotional and physical perspective but also in the development of their relationship with the new setting and other stakeholders. The chapter argued that parents should be seen as co-constructors with learners and practitioners in ensuring successful transitions.

Rationale

This chapter explores practitioner perceptions of transition and the role that they play in instigating and facilitating that process, by structuring the environment for new learners, developing meaningful relationships and communicating effectively. This is in order to ensure that the transition is constructive and allows for both personal and academic growth in the learner. Practitioners are responsible for the instigation and control of procedures around transition and can be perceived as the agents of change. The receiving setting usually works in collaboration with its feeder schools/settings when organising the timing of transition events and activities. The fundamental purpose of the transition process is to ensure that the incoming cohort is familiar with the main features of the new setting (such as the environment and location) and that it is prepared for the forthcoming transition in terms of expectations and arrangements. The practitioner role is of critical importance because there is a clear connection between transition, health and well-being (Fane et al, 2016). If transition is not conducted effectively, Fane et al (2016) suggest it can have a negative impact on an individual's ability to learn in the new environment. It is therefore vital that practitioners are aware of the significance of transition activities upon individuals and that they reflect upon this in order to ensure that expectation of change among new learners is realistic and accepted. In this context, practitioners should be expected to not only work directly with learners but also to *promote respectful cooperation with families in order to understand each other's often conflicting reasons and motives, and move in the same direction in supporting students, especially at transition points*' (Cuconato et al, 2015, p 313).

With this in mind, views from a range of practitioners are interspersed in the chapter to support points from certain perspectives:

- preparation – what practitioners do in preparation for the new cohort of learners;
- process – the processes that facilitate the transition from a practitioner perspective;
- outcome – how practitioners perceive the effectiveness of the transition process and the impact upon future transitions.

Preparing for transition

Practitioners play a vital role in the preparation and organisation of activities and events that guide and facilitate the transition process. In early years environments there is much discussion around the concept of school readiness, which is the process by which the child is prepared for the transition from preschool to school (Puccioni, 2015). School readiness is *'generally understood as the assessment of children's development prior to and during the transition to school'* (Fane et al, 2016, p 127). While parents/carers have a pivotal role to play in early learning, it is high-quality preschool settings that are critical in providing a solid foundation for the transition to more formal schooling (Packer et al, 2018). Readiness for transition is important for the child not only because it ensures engagement with the process but also because it means that the individual is able to settle into the new environment with minimum disruption. Practitioners are critical here. They must understand how and when to commence this process as well as initiating the building of connections among various participants in the transition cycle. As Tobbell and O'Donnell (2013, p 17) state, from the beginning of the transition process practitioners are the *'powerbrokers in a community [who] actively encourage practices which invite participation, and thus facilitate the formation of interpersonal relationships, making new members feel welcome and secure'*. Therefore for a successful transition, practitioners need to ensure preparation is thorough.

One way to ensure an effective transition is to facilitate initial activities that are relatively informal. For example, learners can attend the new setting to see a particular event prior to starting there, or the new setting can be used for feeder setting activities. An example of such an activity is:

- *... getting to know you* (P, Year 2),

which provides an opportunity for learners to become familiar with aspects of the school environment as a preparation for later transition. A similar approach is seen in another setting.

- *We decided to offer sessions to Year 4... to do CSI Science. The intention is to develop science skills, they solve a crime... it's an opportunity for [learners] to know who the headteacher is, who we are and also an opportunity for them to see the laboratories, which is something different for them* (HoY, secondary school 1).

As well as enabling familiarity with the environment it also introduces key practitioners. This way pupils experience aspects of setting without an explicit focus on the transition itself. Such activities can also enable learners to feel comfortable about entering and exploring aspects of the new place, before they have to consider their own place in it.

- *We set up 'walk abouts' so they can be introduced to the setting and go up and view all the different departments* (P, FE college 1).
- *At playtimes when the big yard is free, the Nursery children come up with the current Nursery staff and they play on the new yard to get used to it* (P, Year 2).

Another important preparation for an effective transition for the practitioner is to be aware at the beginning of the needs and demands of the incoming cohort. This is particularly significant for practitioners because they *'educate in complex societies and encounter students with increasingly uneven resources, skills and cultural backgrounds'* (Cuconato et al, 2015, p 311). If practitioners are, therefore, to be agents of change, they must be flexible and reflective in order to work successfully with all learners, particularly those who might present with increasingly complex challenges (as discussed in Chapter 3).

Process: crossing the bridge

In conceptualising the process of transition, Huser et al (2016) draw upon the metaphor of a bridge, referring to the creation of a number of bridges that can be used to cross the one river (the move from one setting to another). In using this comparison to understand some of the complexities of the transition process, the practitioner's role is to enable the construction of a number of 'bridges' and provide opportunities for a range of *crossings*. This can be organised in a variety of ways as evidenced by responses from practitioners.

- *Currently I have got Nursery children coming over every day through the week in little groups so they come once a week for half an hour* (P, Reception 1).

These short but frequent sessions are considered effective for particularly young learners as there is an opportunity for them to become familiar with the new environment.

- *We have a changeover morning… when they go up to see their new class* (P, Reception 1).

In addition, there are opportunities for practitioners in the receiving settings to visit learners in their own environment.

- *We have some contact with the comprehensive schools with Year 10s. We go in and see them, we keep in touch through taster days so once they have applied they can come in* (P, FE college 2).

This is one way that practitioners are able to approach transition through the lens of communities of practice. With this approach, there is a stress on learning as a community activity, where the learner becomes a part of that community through the facilitation of the practitioner, the activities undertaken and the community itself (Tobbell and O'Donnell, 2005). The practitioner's role is essential in this – providing a bridge so that learners can join the communities successfully. As Sutherland et al (2010, p 37) note, *'close liaison will ensure that joint planning can take place around transition and the transfer of both "hard" and "soft" data can easily be facilitated'*. Whichever bridge is chosen to traverse from one setting to another, the route they take needs to be guided, supported and smoothed.

PRACTITIONERS AS FACILITATORS

While practitioners in the setting receiving new learners are key to the facilitation of a smooth transition, the feeder setting also has an important role to play. Information from the feeder setting enables practitioners to ensure appropriate foundations are laid. They receive information about the needs of the new learners, their environment, experiences and expectations. This means practitioners can organise transitions effectively and support (if needed) can be put in place. This understanding can be gained both formally and informally. The information perceived as relevant can vary from setting to setting and according to the age of the learners. For example, according to Correia and Marquez-Pinto's (2016) study on teachers' perspectives on how children adapt to school, practitioners had varying perspectives of what makes transition successful. Preschool teachers placed emphasis on the motivation to learn, while primary-school teachers focused more upon learner behaviours (for example self-control and self-regulation). This resonates with Huser et al's (2016) assertion that the bridge needs to be bi-directional, that there needs to be clear understanding of expectations and outcomes between settings and between the practitioners and the learners.

PRACTITIONERS AS PARTNERS

Ensuring the successful crossing of the transition *bridge* relies upon the shared professional stance practitioners have in each setting and the relationships that begin to forge as learners move from one setting to another. Many practitioners feel that transition has a wider remit, with a value in developing resilience in learners not only at the educational point of transition, but during their life journey.

· *Transitions are one of the most important elements that we need to be working on with our children. It is that resilience within our children and transitions can be not just moving rooms and schools it can be the arrival of a new baby, it can be the breakdown of family, divorce, bereavement; so there are different ways that we need to prepare our children in their lives and it's how we respond to those transitions* (P, Year 2).

This relates to the communities of practice theory whereby practitioners draw upon their own experiences to enhance the competencies of the transition process (Wenger-Trayner and Wenger-Trayner, 2015). A project undertaken in Germany recognised key factors that strengthened the connections between kindergarten and primary schools (Huser et al, 2016). These included: providing opportunities for establishing a shared understanding and approach in the process of transition from both the receiving setting and the feeder setting; and supporting ongoing project work between settings so that there is a potential to cement ties. Practitioners in the feeder settings need to have an understanding of the new environment and the educational demands that will be made upon their learners so that they can prepare and support appropriately.

- *On days when we are not using our classroom... Nursery practitioners will bring groups of pupils up into our environment. Then they get 10 or 15 minutes play... to get used to the transition* (P, Year 1).

This is further evidence of the *bridge* being bi-directional with practitioners physically making a connection between the feeder and the receiving setting.

As the time of transition draws near, practitioners with key roles in transition work more closely with the feeder settings, particularly from preschool to other settings. This is on both an informal and formal level.

- *We pass over all the records to each other as staff too and have official and unofficial chats about all the children... The Nursery staff also go out at the start of term to visit Nursery children in their homes. They go in twos so they get to know the new children before they start* (P, Year 2).
- *I collect data on the individuals with feeder settings and discuss ability, interests, traits, history, needs, safeguarding etc... I create a passport for each child for the form teacher... [which] includes test results, teacher comments, attendance, parent comments and a photo... it helps to get to know the children* (HoY, secondary school 1).

Closer to the time of transition this can involve ensuring that learners are with their friendship groups in the new environment.

- *In the summer term I visit the schools and ask the pupils to write down the names of three friends... they are guaranteed to have one friend in their form class* (HoY, secondary school 2).

As well as working in partnership with practitioners, there has to be a sense of partnership between the learners themselves.

- *The importance of developing communication-friendly spaces for learners is important in this process and in transition as a whole* (P, Reception 1).

This reflects Jarman's (2008) concept of the importance of practitioners regarding the environment from the learner's perspective.

- *The environment is really important to us... they transition a lot easier when the environment is familiar to them* (P, Year 2).

This approach helps learners develop a sense of belonging and fosters identification with the new setting in learners.

- *On the last transition day we tell them that over the summer they are representing our school* (HoY, secondary school 2).

PRACTITIONERS SUPPORTING LEARNERS AS FACILITATORS

While learners do not return to their feeder setting in an educational context, consideration must be given by practitioners to the importance of learners being able to either return or at least revisit aspects of their previous setting. This could be through organised visits to the school to speak with the next cohort, or participation in joint activities such as concerts and school trips. Some examples are given here.

- *Our current level 3 students have been working with prospective students and giving them a flavour of the courses we offer through practical activities* (P, FE college 2).
- *Bac[calureate] pupils lead some of the sessions… they have to plan and lead sessions* (HoY, secondary school 1).

Being able to reconnect with former settings provides opportunities for individual reflection and enables learners to draw upon their own experiences to support fellow peers as they embark on their own journeys of transition. This provides an acknowledgement of the relation of earlier phases of life to later phases, linking to life-course theory (Elder Jr et al, 2003). However, as Cuconato et al (2015, p 314) note, this is often not a consideration contemplated by practitioners who if *'not provided with knowledge of the life-course aspects of education and trained to accompany students during transitions are unlikely to feel responsible for the task'*. This is particularly true of older learners who move from secondary school to further-education colleges.

STRUCTURING THE ENVIRONMENT

During the process of transition it is important that learners can begin to identify with the new setting, for example, by encouraging pupils to wear the new setting's uniform during transition events:

- *… so they feel part of the school from day one* (P, Reception 1).

Rice et al (2015), in recording the journey of approximately 2000 pupils moving from primary to secondary school in South East England, noted that identifying positively with the academic and behavioural expectations of the new school and having a sense of belonging was evidence of a successful transition. Another way to do this is by providing opportunities for 'overlap', such as attending a residential course for learners in both the feeder and receiving setting. This offers an opportunity for continuity and familiarity. As the HoY of a secondary school notes:

- *we have a residential week with the feeder schools and Year 7 so I have regular contact with the teachers* (HOY, secondary school 1).

This acknowledges Bronfenbrenner's (1979) ecological systems theory in developing the individual's mesosystem that there is a conscious awareness by practitioners of the interaction between elements of the microsystem. The individual is able to draw upon previous knowledge and understanding and to apply it in the new environment. As a practitioner states:

- *we have five to six transition days each focusing on a different aspect of school life, a day for the core subjects, a day for PE, a day for the other subjects and two other days which focus on the pupils getting to know each other and becoming familiar with the school layout* (P, secondary school 2).

This approach can serve to reduce the fear of the unknown and to alleviate any concerns or anxieties the learner might have (Correia and Marques-Pinto, 2016). In addition, it can also be a means of introducing the learner to the routines of the new setting.

Tobbell and O'Donnell (2013, p 14) state that during the process of transition, *'it may be that the role of the student changes but the student does not necessarily understand this'*. The learner may not realise that on entering the new setting expectations and demands change. Sometimes this needs to be made explicit to learners so that:

- *pupils can see how the school works and what our standards are... and to know our expectations... basic things* (HoY, secondary school 2).

If this is not communicated clearly in the transition process then difficulties may arise. Learners may struggle to identify with the new setting which can lead to issues with engagement and social and emotional well-being and can subsequently impact upon academic progress. Transition activities therefore need to accommodate for the pupil according to individual need.

- *I have made a little book... with photographs for one child because Mum thought he might find transition difficult so wanted a book with staff photos... so he has taken it home today* (P, Reception 1).

Outcome: clarifying expectations

As identified earlier in the chapter clarifying setting expectations and providing an opportunity for exploration and discussion prior to and during the transition process is a key part of a successful transition. It is also important because it can promote the development of positive interpersonal relationships between practitioners and learners. Therefore a consistent practitioner approach and constructive dialogue around the markers of the new setting are critical in terms of setting expectations and standards.

- *We need to get to know the learners and they need to get to know us before they start* (P, FE college 1).
- *Setting expectations is very important as [pupils] know exactly what they should be doing* (P, secondary school 2).

Practitioners also need to look at this from the learner's perspective as they move from one setting to another. This is because their *'social networks are disrupted and students need to make new friends and integrate into a new, larger and more complex social environment, while coping with the loss of some of their elementary school friends'* (Coelho and Romão, 2017, p 86). Building upon an element of familiarity can provide a foundation on which to mitigate the possible negative impact of this disruption. When learners enter the new environment and prospective new community, they are actively assessing it for information so that they can construct understanding (Tobbell and O'Donnell, 2013). This is why there needs to be a focus on establishing the new setting's expectations and routines so that learners are prepared when they become full members of the new setting and supports Vygotsky's (1978) sociocultural theory of cognitive development as the learner is learning from the practitioner. However it is also important that elements of the learner's previous environment are maintained, for example keeping the learner's peers together in a group after the transition process (Correia and Marques-Pinto, 2016).

This connects to life-course theory as *'learning cannot be isolated from the learner's sociocultural environment'* (Miravet and Garcia, 2013, p 1375) and should be a consideration for younger learners where practitioners visit the home prior to the learner starting formally at the setting. Despite this Cuconato et al (2015, p 317) note in their study on practitioners' perceptions of their role in transition:

many teachers we interviewed admitted that they do not have extensive knowledge of either the family or the neighbourhood in which their students live outside school.

When practitioners do promote positive social interaction with learners, they able to facilitate learner engagement and enable identification with the new setting. This is *'school connectedness'* (Waters et al, 2014) and is *'one of the most important predictors of adolescent health, social and academic outcomes'* (ibid, p 544). This is supported by Lizzio et al (2011) who argue that the greater the identification the learner has with the setting, the greater their motivation is to engage with learning. While initial links with the learner's family and community might not necessarily happen, opportunities for practitioner–learner social interaction are evidenced via the extra-curricular and residential activities organised by settings. Active social interaction promotion by practitioners can be of particular value for learners who are experiencing difficulties in their educational journey and who may require intensive support and intervention (Carmen et al, 2010).

PRACTITIONER-LEARNER RELATIONSHIPS

Effective relationships between learners and practitioners are central to learner participation in transition. Tobbell and O'Donnell (2013, p 11) argue that *'interpersonal relationships are a pre-requisite to learning relationships'* and that there should be a focus in settings on providing opportunities for the development of interpersonal relationships in addition to teaching. The quality of these relationships specifically (and relationships in general) is pivotal in ensuring successful learning and social development and can have an influence on the way in which future relationships are formed (Bronfenbrenner, 1979). Iruka et al (2010), in their study on the relationships between children and their mothers and teachers in kindergarten, found a positive correlation between the quality of the pupil–teacher relationships and successful academic and social trajectories during primary schooling. Lizzio et al (2011) further support this in noting the importance of learners' perceptions of positive relationships with practitioners in enhancing both academic success and enhanced social functioning. These relationships can facilitate greater learner engagement in the process and identification with the new setting, which ensures a smooth transition. Constructive communication and dialogue between practitioner and learner help identify key markers of the new setting and are seen as critical in terms of identifying the setting's (and the learner's) expectations and standards (Tobbell and O'Donnell, 2013).

- *We have a starting school pack in Nursery when they come to the open day. They have a little booklet when they start about PE etc. We also have photos of the staff in the open-day booklet too. They have a self-registration ticket with a picture which they familiarise themselves with over the holidays so when they come in September they know where to hang their bags and coats as their peg will have the same picture as the self-registration ticket. They also have 'meet the teacher' sessions so the parents and children can get used to us* (P, Reception 1).

This is also a feature in FE settings, and provides opportunities for practitioners to meet with learners and to answer any questions they might have before committing to the course. At this point in the process, their early interactions provide learners with an opportunity to have a flavour of the new setting.

The practitioner–learner relationship is further developed when the new intake first enters the setting. Orientation activities organised by practitioners allow for a relationship to develop with the learners and vice versa, as well as serving to support learners in becoming more familiar with the environment and expectations.

- *In the first week, we do 'getting to know each other' activities. They write their name in front of them and then they have to say something about themselves so it is like an icebreaker* (P, FE college 1).
- *[They bring] a picture of themselves or their families so we get to know the children. It is nice to sit down, talk to them, and work with them to find out names and make it a positive time. We tell them a little bit about what to expect* (P, Year 2).

In line with theory surrounding communities of learning, these dialogues and processes not only develop relationships between practitioners, learners, families and communities, but they also provide opportunity for the building of practitioner expertise while also recognising the expertise of others (Wallis and Dockett, 2015). Developing good practitioner–learner interpersonal relationships at this point of transition also enables the establishment of effective learning relationships, and so passage through the zone of proximal development (ZPD) as identified by Vygotsky (1978).

Focus on positive practitioner–learner relationships is therefore vital for effective transitions because it can have a significant impact on their social and emotional health outcomes, such as improved peer relationships, better educational success and a reduced chance of participation in risky behaviours (Waters et al, 2014; Corriea and Marquez-Pinto, 2016). It is important to note that to be successful, these relationships are also dependent other key factors: effective relationships between practitioners from all settings involved; the use of strategies to promote the learning environment; and the development of a sense of belonging among learners (Huser et al, 2016).

Consistent approaches

Central to effective transition is the consistency of application. In general, the younger the learner the fewer practitioners they encounter, and therefore a consistent approach is more easily achieved. Younger learners tend also to remain in the same environments for longer periods of time. Consistency with regards to expectations is central to maintaining the interpersonal relationships between practitioner and learner. As learners become older they may interact with a wide number of practitioners whose expectations with regards to rules and expectations may vary considerably from practitioner to practitioner. While Tobbell and O'Donnell (2013) acknowledge that learners can accommodate the differing demands made upon learners by practitioners, this variation in approach initially can be quite stressful to learners and can add to the burden of transition. To alleviate this, a focus upon reiterating expectations of the new setting to learners ensures a consensus of understanding and consistent approach.

School–home relationships

While the transition process can be viewed from the learner–practitioner perspective, these relationships are also influenced by those with other key stakeholders in the process, such as parents/carers. These relationships are critical and so consideration of them is needed. Open days or evenings are often used as a means of allowing learners and their parents to explore the new setting and provide a first point of contact for parents.

- *We have an open evening... a Nursery and Reception new-intake meeting. Where we talk about the things we are doing... Literally, the parents just want to know who their teacher will be and if there is any support staff* (P, Year 2).
- *For Nursery children coming into the Nursery we do have parents in for a meeting. We try to talk to all the children too on that open afternoon so we can get to know them. We put out lots of activities so it is like it would be on a normal school day so the children can get used to us and the classroom* (P, Reception 1).

Ensuring that communication channels are effective and that parents are aware of how to contact or to interact with settings is important in enabling the learner to adapt to the next educational context and for maximising the learner's growth potential (Correia and Marquez-Pinto, 2016).

PRACTITIONER DISCOURSE

- *We have an evening of sharing information for Year 6 pupils in July. They receive an information pack but we are developing a transition website with links that parents can access...* (P, secondary school 2).
- *We used to communicate via Year 6 teachers but have had to adapt... We send letters and have a school Twitter account just for Transition where all information is tweeted... It allows parents to follow events at the school and to see the successes* (HoY, secondary school 1).

Effective communication serves to alleviate concerns and potential anxiety about the transition experience. This is particularly true as the learner becomes older and there is increasing emphasis on taking responsibility and becoming more independent. Meetings to discuss expectations, the setting as an organisation, educational practices and curriculum delivery facilitate the process of transition from a parental perspective and in turn enable appropriate support for learners. A wide array of activities evidenced from the practitioners interviewed involve key stakeholders in addition to learners in the transition process, such as open days, meetings with practitioners, or opportunities to experience aspects of the school day.

The development of relationships with stakeholders should be ongoing, to further support learners as they begin to settle into their new environment.

- *Sessions for parents are organised during the first term on literacy, numeracy, well-being and e-safety... They also have an opportunity to meet with their child's tutor and SEN department if they want to... We also have a 'settling-in evening' at the beginning of November... Parents meet with the class tutor who... provides general feedback... The residential trip in November for Year 7 brings the transition to a close as pupils are usually quite settled by then* (HoY, secondary school 1).

Responding to feedback

Practitioners generally consider that the activities they have put in place are sufficient but regularly seek feedback from learners and parents with regards to the transition process.

- *We ask them [learners] do they have everything they need for the course... We have learner voice and a questionnaire they fill in asking them how induction went etc* (P, FE college 2).
- *They do a self-report where they draw a picture of what they liked in Nursery and they draw a picture of what they would like to do in Reception which is shared with the new teacher* (P, Reception 1).
- *We have had so many parents asking this year if we could [have] a more formalised open afternoon or an open session where children and their parents can come and stay and play in the Reception environment* (P, Year 1).

Feedback from learners and key stakeholders reflects amendments made to the transition process in order to secure the best outcome for learners. Concerns raised by parents are incorporated into the transition events, for example:

- *we invited parents in at lunchtime... They could either bring a packed lunch and stay and eat it with the children or they could experience the school dinner. This was a really good opportunity as very often it is the lunchtime they [parents] were most worried about* (P, Year 1).

As a consequence of feedback given to settings, practices are changed or amended.

- *One afternoon wasn't enough for us, so we have introduced the longer transitions over the last two years [Nursery to Reception]* (P, Year 2).
- *We work well together as a team and we sit down and reflect on what certain people have done during induction week and we think oh that's a good idea and we share best practice* (P, FE college 1).

This demonstrates that the transition process is not a static one but rather is fluid, responding to the changing needs of new learners. This is not only from the learner perspective, but also includes parental feedback. Encouraging more active parental involvement in the learner's journey is also a consideration for practitioners in settings with older learners.

- *We haven't really done a lot with parents. That is something we need to develop in the future. However, before coming to us they usually do come with their parents so they do get the information. We do send out consent forms so we do have ongoing consent from parents for trips etc... I have spoken to numerous parents over the years if there is any problem with the learners and I usually build up a rapport with that parent so they will come in or we will speak over the phone* (P, FE college 1).

Recommendations

Analysing responses from practitioners has highlighted a number of key features that need consideration in planning for transition, namely:

- the importance of preparing learners appropriately for the forthcoming change;
- fostering a sense of identity and belonging in the new setting; and
- developing effective interpersonal relationships between practitioner and learner so that a positive learning environment is created from the outset.

While practitioners are familiar with the process of transition and have developed effective strategies to support learners, it is important to note the value of reflection in effecting positive transition activities and to tailor transition practice according to the learner. In realising this, practitioners need to develop a cross-setting approach and recognise the value of both the learner and stakeholder voice in enhancing the quality of the transition process.

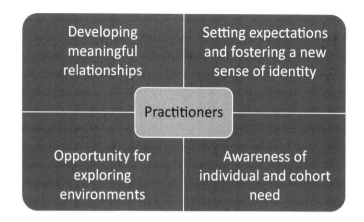

Figure 6.1 Recommendations for practitioners in ensuring effective transition experiences

Conclusion

The importance of the role practitioners take in transition cannot be underestimated. Effective planning, smooth co-ordination of activities and meaningful relationships with parents, learners and stakeholders all impact on the success of the transition process. It is important that practitioners recognise the importance of developing a relationship with learners so that they are equipped for the process of transition and ready to engage with learning in the new setting both cognitively and emotionally (Sutherland et al, 2010).

❖ Reflective questions

1. What have you learnt about the practitioner role in the transition process?

2. Drawing upon your own experience, how effective are the transition practices in your own setting?

3. How could you use feedback from learners and key stakeholders to inform transition practices in your setting?

4. When preparing for transition, what considerations would you take in to account from the perspective of learners?

5. How can both academic and social transitions be considered to support the learner?

Suggested reading

Tobbell, J and O'Donnell, V L (2013) The Formation of Interpersonal and Learning Relationships in the Transition From Primary to Secondary School: Students, Teachers and School Context. *International Journal of Educational Research*, 59: 11–23.

Using an ethnographic method this study explores the value of developing effective interpersonal and learning relationships with learners to support effective transition from primary to secondary school.

Wilder, J and Lillvist, A (2018) Learning Journey: A Conceptual Framework for Analyzing Children's Learning in Educational Transitions. *European Early Childhood Education Research Journal*, 26(5): 688–700. [online] Available at: https://doi.org/10.1080/1350293X.2018.1522736 (accessed 13 June 2020).

This article discusses the concept of the 'learning journey' in analysing children's learning in early educational transitions and proposes a model for effective practice.

Huser, C, Dockett, S and Perry, B (2016) Transition to School: Revisiting the Bridge Metaphor. *European Early Childhood Education Research Journal*, 24(3): 439–49. [online] Available at: http://dx.doi.org/10.1080/1350293X.2015.1102414 (accessed 24 May 2020).

This article explores the bridge metaphor in transition drawing upon theories of rites of passage, and the application of this in ensuring successful educational transitions.

References

Bronfenbrenner, U (1979) *The Ecology of Human Development: Experiments by Nature and Design*. Boston, MA: Harvard University Press.

Carmen, B, Waycott, L and Smith, K (2010) Rock Up: An Initiative Supporting Students' Wellbeing in Their Transition to Secondary School. *Children and Youth Services Review*, 33: 167–72.

Coelho, V A and Romão, A M (2017) The Impact of Secondary School Transition on Self-Concept and Self-Esteem. *Revista de Psicodidáctica*, 22(2): 85–92.

Correia, K and Marques-Pinto, A (2016) Adaptation in the Transition to School: Perspectives of Parents, Preschool and Primary School Teachers. *Educational Research*, 58(3): 247–64. [online] Available at: https://doi.org/10.1080/00131881.2016.1200255 (accessed 7 June 2020).

Cuconato, M, du Bois-Reymond, M and Lunabba, H (2015) Between Gate-Keeping and Support: Teachers' Perception of Their Role in Transition. *International Journal of Qualitative Studies in Education*, 28(3): 311–28. [online] Available at: https://doi.org/10.1080/09518398.2014.987854 (accessed 7 June 2020).

Elder Jr, G H, Johnson, M K and Crosnoe, R (2003) The Emergence and Development of Life Course Theory. In Mortimer, J T and Shanahan, M J (eds) *Handbook of the Life Course*. New York: Kluwer Academic/Plenum Publishers.

Fane, J, MacDoughall, C, Redmond, G, Jovanovic, J and Ward, P (2016) Young Children's Health and Wellbeing Across the Transition to School: A Critical Interpretive Synthesis. *Children Australia*, 41(2): 125–40. [online] Available at: https://doi.org/10.1017/cha.2016.4 (accessed 7 June 2020).

Huser, C, Dockett, S and Perry, B (2016) Transition to School: Revisiting the Bridge Metaphor. *European Early Childhood Education Research Journal*, 24(3): 439–49. [online] Available at: http://dx.doi.org/10.1080/1350293X.2015.1102414 (accessed 7 June 2020).

Iruka, I U, Burchinal, M and Cai, K (2010) Long-Term Effect of Early Relationships for African American Children's Academic and Social Development: An Examination From Kindergarten to Fifth Grade. *Journal of Black Psychology*, 36(2): 144–71.

Jarman, E (2008) Creating Spaces That Are 'Communication Friendly'. *Mathematics Teaching Incorporating Micromath*, 209: 31–3.

Lizzio, A, Dempster, N and Neumann, R (2011) Pathways to Formal and Informal Student Leadership: The Influence of Peer and Teacher-Student Relationships and Level of School Identification on Students' Motivations. *International Journal of Leadership in Education*, 14(1): 85–102. [online] Available at: https://doi.org/10.1080/13603124.2010.482674 (accessed 7 June 2020).

Miravet, L M and Garcia, O M (2013) The Role of Teachers' Shared Values and Objectives in Promoting Intercultural and Inclusive School Cultures: A Case Study. *International Journal of Qualitative Studies in Education*, 26(10): 1373–86. [online] Available at: https://doi.org/10.1080/09518398.2012.731535 (accessed 7 June 2020).

Packer, R, Watkins, P and Hughes, M (2018) Playing with Words: Becoming a Reader and a Writer. In McInnes, K and Thomas, A (eds) *Teaching Early Years*. London: Sage.

Puccioni, J (2015) Parents' Conceptions of School Readiness, Transition Practices and Children's Academic Achievement Trajectories. *The Journal of Educational Research*, 108: 130–47. [online] Available at: https://doi.org/10.1080/00220671.2013.850399 (accessed 7 June 2020).

Rice, F, Frederickson, N, Shelton, K, McManus, C, Riglin, L and Ng-Knight, T (2015) Identifying Factors That Predict Successful and Difficult Transitions to Secondary School. [online] Available at: https://nuffieldfoundation.org/wp-content/uploads/2019/11/STARS_report.pdf (accessed 7 June 2020).

Sutherland, R, Ching Yee, W, McNess, E and Harris, R (2010) *Supporting Learning in the Transition From Primary to Secondary Schools*. Bristol: University of Bristol. [online] Available at: https://bristol.ac.uk/media-library/sites/cmpo/documents/transition.pdf (accessed 7 June 2020).

Tobbell, J and O'Donnell, V L (2005) Theorising Educational Transitions, Communities, Practice and Participation. In *Conference on Sociocultural Theory in Educational Research and Practice*. University of Manchester (Unpublished).

Tobbell, J and O'Donnell, V L (2013) The Formation of Interpersonal and Learning Relationships in the Transition From Primary to Secondary School: Students, Teachers and School Context. *International Journal of Educational Research*, 59: 11– 23.

Vygotsky, L (1978) *Mind in Society. The Development of Higher Psychological Processes.* Cambridge, MA: Harvard University Press.

Wallis, J and Dockett, S (2015) Stakeholders, Networks and Links in Early Childhood Policy: Network Analysis and the Transition to School: Position Statement. *Contemporary Issues in Early Childhood*, 16(4): 339–54.

Waters, S, Lester, L and Cross, D (2014) How Does Support From Peers Compare With Support From Adults as Students Transition to Secondary School? *Journal of Adolescent Health*, 54: 543–9.

Wenger-Traynor, E and Wenger-Traynor, B (2015) Introduction to Communities of Practice: A Brief Overview of the Concept and Its Uses. [online] Available at: https://wenger-trayner.com/introduction-to-communities of practice/ (accessed 13 June 2020).

7. INTERNATIONAL PERSPECTIVES ON TRANSITIONS

Recap

The previous chapters have discussed different aspects that are important to understanding key debates in transition and what can affect transitions in a UK context. This chapter is an introduction to transitions from an international perspective. As the previous chapters demonstrate, transitions can be a number of things (challenging, mandatory, necessary) and involve a range of stakeholders. Ecclestone et al (2010) stress the importance of being aware of how concepts of transition are interpreted from different cultural, political and pedagogical frameworks. Lally and Doyle (2012) encourage a new conversation about how we view transitions and how we can best use international perspectives. This chapter gives an overview of learner experiences of some international approaches to transition and therefore provides an international lens through which transitions can be viewed. The Organisation for Economic Co-operation and Development (OECD, 2019a) provides excellent 'education at a glance' profiles by country on an annual basis and these are a good starting point to help understand the context of an education system and what may impact on transitions.

Rationale

Using Bronfenbrenner's ecological systems approach (1979, 1989) as a framework, this chapter explores some of the commonalities and differences of how transitions are approached in a global context as well as the scaffolds put in place to support children and young people through them. This is important because an understanding of transition approaches in a global context can be used to inform discussions on policy development, learner development, stakeholder voice and curriculum design. Bronfenbrenner's (1979, 1989) model is particularly useful in this context because of its ability to illustrate the complexity and range of transitions that a learner may encounter on their learning journey. Using Bronfenbrenner's macrosystem as a framework, exploration of approaches in Europe (with reference to other countries to support the ideas) are presented. For more specific examples of practice the meso- and microsystems are referenced. The chapter is based on a review of the literature, international reports and conversations with learners and teachers from different countries about their experiences. Four areas of focus were identified and are reflected in the chapter:

- different starting ages for compulsory education;
- readiness for transition from a learner, school and parent perspective;
- pedagogies of educational transitions and their influences;
- context – environment, policy and culture.

Transition experiences

The ways in which a learner is required to engage with compulsory education and make transitions is different across the world. In order to understand the different stages and transition points, it is important to be familiar with global classification of the different stages of compulsory education using the International Standard Classification of Education (ISCED) (UNESCO, 2012). Table 7.1 is a summary of the main classifications.

Table 7.1 International Standard Classifications of Education to end of compulsory education cycle

CLASSIFICATION	STAGE	DEFINITION
ISCED 0	Early years	Early childhood programmes that have an intentional education component that are for children under three years old.
ISCED 1	Primary education	Entry age is normally 3–7 to establish a solid foundation for learning and understanding core areas of knowledge and personal and social development (with a focus on literacy and numeracy).
ISCED 2	Lower-secondary education	Typically 10–13 years of age.
ISCED 3	Upper-secondary education	Programmes at this level are typically designed to complete secondary education in preparation for tertiary education or provide skills relevant to employment, or both. Pupils enter this level typically between the ages of 14 and 16.

Table 7.1 makes it possible to identify at least four transition points as a learner moves through their particular compulsory education system. However, how a country manages and supports the learner journey varies and this can have an effect on the transition experience and the choices available for the learner.

Spotlight on the European experience

According to the European Commission/EACEA/Eurydice (2018) there are 43 education systems, covering 38 countries, and transition into compulsory education ranges from the ages of 3–7. In France the starting age changed to three years old in 2019, while in Sweden, the starting age is seven years old.

INTERNATIONAL PERSPECTIVES ON TRANSITIONS

As a comparison, the starting age in England, Wales and Scotland is five years old. The map in Figure 7.1 provides a sense of the profile of starting ages with 5 and 6 years old being the two most dominant starting ages.

Figure 7.1 When do children start school in Europe?
Source: European Commission/EACEA/Eurydice (2018)

In these education systems age is the only condition for entry into mainstream education. Fourteen education systems (Bulgaria, Ireland, Northern Ireland, Spain, France, Malta, Romania, Scotland, England, Wales, Albania, Iceland, North Macedonia and Turkey) do not allow pupils to defer entry to mainstream school once the starting age is reached. However, in the others, a deferral is possible at the request of parents or possibly at the suggestion of the early years setting, if they consider that a child is not ready to start primary education (European Commission, 2018b). This decision to defer is based on policy that relates to a child's achievement of developmental milestones and is only granted where it is in the best interests of the child. This is explored in more detail later in this chapter in the section on 'readiness' for compulsory education at the start and its different transition points.

STRUCTURES OF COMPULSORY EDUCATION IN EUROPE

The European Commission/EACEA/Eurydice (2018) identifies three main organisational models of primary and lower-secondary education (ISCED 1 and ISCED 2), which are a part of *compulsory education in all European Systems'* (p 5). The models each have an impact on transition points and choices and paths that learners can take. Table 7.2 provides further information on these models.

Table 7.2 Models of compulsory education in Europe (European Commission/EACEA/ Eurydice, 2018)

MODEL	DESCRIPTION	COUNTRIES
Single-structure education	This model provides compulsory schooling throughout with no transition between primary and secondary education. General education is provided for all pupils.	Norway, Sweden, Finland, Denmark, Iceland, Poland, Bulgaria, Albania, Serbia, Bosnia and Herzegovina, Kosovo, North Macedonia, Croatia and Slovenia
Common core curriculum	Once primary education has been completed, all students progress to secondary. All follow a core curriculum.	England, Scotland, Wales, Northern Ireland, Ireland, Italy, Greece, France, Portugal, Estonia, Belgium, Turkey, Romania
Differentiated branches	After completion of primary education, students follow distinct educational pathways. Some countries offer vocational, technical or general education tracks.	Germany, Lithuania, Switzerland, Austria, Netherlands

There are four exceptions: Latvia, Czech Republic, Slovakia and Hungary, where a single structure is the dominant model, although between the ages of 10 and 13, pupils can move to different establishments that offer both a lower-secondary and upper-secondary education (European Commission/EACEA/Eurydice, 2018).

SINGLE-STRUCTURE EDUCATION

It is mainly the Scandinavian countries that follow a single-structure model which can eliminate some of the transition points that are seen in other models. There are learning environments which support learners from 3–16 and schools that offer the same environment from primary to lower-secondary with a home room, often with the same teacher. This is in contrast to school systems, which require significant locational and environmental change. For example in the home nations of the United Kingdom, pupils move from a small primary school to a large secondary school at the age of 11. This transition typically exposes pupils to a new social and structural environment, whereas students in Sweden mostly remain in the same school and class all the way through primary and secondary school.

Examples from Sweden and Denmark

Early childhood education is available to children from one to five years of age. There is an emphasis on the importance of play in a child's development and learning, as well as a strong focus on understanding and incorporating the interests and needs of children into their preschool experience. This means that although children do not start compulsory education until seven years old there are opportunities to ensure that they are prepared for the transition into compulsory education in terms of development and social interaction. A UK exchange student whose three-year-old daughter experienced the Swedish system commented on the benefits of the holistic approach to learning.

- *I was worried about the impact of being in a different country with a different language but my daughter was taken into a nurturing environment that developed her confidence through play and listening and in a new language!* (L).

In Sweden, children make the transition from preschool to compulsory school via a preschool class. The preschool class is a voluntary school form for six-year-old children (Ackesjö, 2013) and this can support their readiness for entering compulsory education. Broström (2012) found that preschools have tended to narrow their activities to emphasise school preparation with a focus on teaching in school-related areas. The aim is to support development and learning, and provide a bridge to entering compulsory education, and provides an example of how transition can be supported for the learner, parent and the school.

The compulsory element of education is a single streamlined structure where pupils do not have to worry about physical transitions but continue in the same environment. This approach is also dominant in Denmark. In Denmark, there is no transition from primary to secondary school as the public school system consists of an integrated primary and lower-secondary school (average school size around 400 students) with one year of preschool, nine years of primary and lower-secondary and an optional one-year tenth form (Danish Ministry of Education, 2016, cited in Nielsen et al, 2017).

Not having a change in learning environment can, however, have a negative effect. Pupils remain in the same class with the same classmates with the intention of creating a safe and trustful school class environment. However, for students who do not fit in with the other classmates there is no second chance to be part of a new peer group or have new classmates or to make new friends from a larger group that support their changing needs and interests (Nielsen et al, 2017). The transition to secondary school can also be seen as a step into being more responsible and autonomous. This links with debates about the role of developing resilience in pupils and learner independence and autonomy.

COMMON CORE CURRICULUM

In this model of an education system, pupils, after successful completion of primary education, progress to the lower-secondary level where they follow the same general common core curriculum. This is the model that is adopted in the United Kingdom. Reflections on this type of system and its key transition points are discussed in previous chapters of the book. If you wish to explore other approaches to the common core curriculum outside the UK look at the following countries: Italy; Greece; France; Portugal; Romania; and Estonia.

DIFFERENTIATED BRANCHES

The third model offers different pathways to secondary education based on performance in school combined with a conversation between parent and teacher. After successful completion of primary education, students are required to follow distinct educational pathways or specific types of schooling, either at the beginning or during lower-secondary education, for example vocational, technical or general education (European Commission/EACEA/Eurydice, 2018).

In other European countries there are additional paths, for example in Denmark education attainment consists of transitions where pupils have to think about not only the next higher level but which branch to follow. Larsen et al (2014), in their evaluation of educational attainment in Denmark, explain that the primary and lower-secondary schooling levels are integrated in a compulsory nine-year programme followed by an optional tenth year. The upper-secondary level is divided into two main tracks – vocational education and training (VET) and general upper-secondary education.

Examples from Germany

Early childhood education in Germany is available from 0–6 and is provided in a range of ways including *Kinderkrippen* (crèches), child-minding centres, kindergarten, and day-care centres. For children older than two there are seven areas of learning (Studying in Germany, 2020):

1. language, writing, communication;
2. personal and social development;
3. development of values and religious education;
4. mathematics, natural sciences, (information) technology;
5. fine arts/working with different media;
6. body, movement, health; and
7. nature and cultural environments.

There is a strong emphasis on working with parents. One respondent reflected on their experience:

- *I started kindergarten when I was four years old. The experience was very good and I still remember the lady who looked after me. I liked the structure and environment. I grew up in a large family with six older siblings and it was a very busy home. My parents provided the opportunities but it was up to me to do things* (L1, Germany).

An interview with one parent discussed the role that financial support plays in supporting a child as they transition into compulsory education.

- *There is more financial support for women in Germany to spend time with their child. You can be away from work for up to three years* (L1, Germany).

Grundschule (primary school) ranges from the age of 6 until the completion of grade 4 (or grade 6 in Berlin and Brandenburg). Respondents to a survey carried out for this book commented that the move into primary school was quite low-key. There were no visits. It was *not obvious, not inflated* but *celebrated*.

- *We were welcomed with a present to primary school. Every child was given a cone with sweets and a gift. I can remember I was given an alarm clock!* (L1, Germany).

The transition into secondary school is marked by the *Grundschule* target outcomes. Pupils enter secondary school at ten. There is a range of secondary education options available to learners and this is where the differentiated branches have a potential impact on transition. Table 7.3 below is based on country-based OECD data from the annual *Education at a Glance* report (OECD, 2019a) and details the publicly funded routes.

Table 7.3 identified a strength of the differentiated model in that it offers learners the opportunity to move through education or transition to different pathways that support their strengths and interests. At the end of the primary education a learner's performance is evaluated through looking at academic records, teacher feedback and parent–teacher discussions. Learners are placed on a route to secondary schools that affect their future education options.

- *Not being recommended for a particular route at ten does not restrict your options. I went to a gymnasium which is seen as mainly an academic route but I opted to do an apprenticeship before going to university* (L1, Germany).
- *The vocational route is really valued in Germany and I was able to get real business experience before completing the requirements to get into university. Advice was available to support me with my decisions and the system made it possible to follow options at the right time for me* (L2, Germany).
- *I did not visit the secondary school before I went there. Discussion was had with the teachers and my parents about the best route. I remember doing tests… It was not an issue not visiting the school . Sometimes [it] is better not to have the stories about what it is and artificially inflate what it is* (L1, Germany).

Table 7.3 A general table for primary and secondary education routes in Germany (noting that there are some regional differences)

EDUCATION	SCHOOL/LEVEL	AGE	NUMBER OF YEARS	NOTES
Primary	*Grundschule*	6–10	4	
Primary	*Grundschule*	6–12	6	Berlin and Brandenburg
Secondary	*Hauptschule*	10–15	5	
Secondary	*Realschule*	10–15	6	
Secondary	*Gymnasia*	10–18	8	Strong academic focus
Secondary	*Gesamtschule*	10–15	5	
Secondary	*Berufliches Gymnasium/ Fachgymnasium*	16–19	3	
Secondary	*Höhere Handelsschule* (Commercial College)	17–18	1	
Vocational	Vocational University Maturity Certificate	16–18	2	
Vocational	*Berufsschule* (part-time)	15–18	3	
Vocational	*Gymnasiale Oberstufe* (since 1972)	16–19	3	
Vocational	*Fachschulen*		3	Entry into a profession
Vocational	*Ausbildung*	19–20	2	Apprenticeship

From the respondents, transition seems to be supported in a very pragmatic way where there is an expectation that learners and parents take responsibility to manage the change through different stages.

· *Although you may be put on a certain path you are not prevented from taking higher qualifications at the time that is right for you* (L2, Germany).

All the respondents felt that their transitions were managed in a low-key and matter-of-fact way. The education system appears to provide opportunities to follow paths at a time that is right for the learner. All routes are valued and learners are able to move between paths in a non-linear way. For example learners can engage in a vocational path and later move to a more academic path in preparation for university study. One respondent reflected on her own journey and the options available:

- *I was accepted to study at the gymnasium and followed an academic route but when I completed secondary I had the opportunity to follow an apprenticeship which I did for two years before attending university* (L1, Germany).

Readiness for transitions in education

Within educational research, a number of longitudinal studies have demonstrated superior academic, motivational and well-being outcomes for children who had attended child-initiated, play-based preschool programmes. As pointed out in Chapter 4, the first transition experience a learner has may influence the future experiences of transition (Dunlop, 2003) and their engagement with education. There are 15 education systems in Europe that require proof of readiness for starting compulsory education. There is a common focus on whether the child is emotionally, mentally, psychologically and physically mature enough to cope with the demands of primary education. United Nations Children's Fund (UNICEF, 2012) has very clear guidance on school readiness for the child, school and parent, suggesting a focus on three main factors.

1. *Are all children entering school with the social and cognitive skills and competencies needed to achieve in school?*
2. *Are schools equipped and ready to provide optimal learning environments for all children?*
3. *Are families and communities ready to help their children make a smooth transition into school?*

(UNICEF, 2012, p 3)

A holistic approach should be in place to ensure that all stakeholders (school, pupil and family/caregivers) are part of supporting the transition into school and cannot be looked at separately. Figure 7.2 below demonstrates how readiness for school is an interconnected responsibility and it is critical that all parts work together to ensure successful transitions.

Rouse et al (2005) found that learners who enter school ready to learn and transition smoothly into a primary-school learning environment are more likely to be employed as adults. Some countries do acknowledge that children develop at different rates which supports systems that enable children to defer their entry into the compulsory education system and in some cases at secondary level too. In order for this model to work there must be opportunities for dialogue between parents and school. For example in Germany, educators discuss progression with parents who together agree on measures for the development of a child's learning skills and whether they are ready for compulsory school attendance.

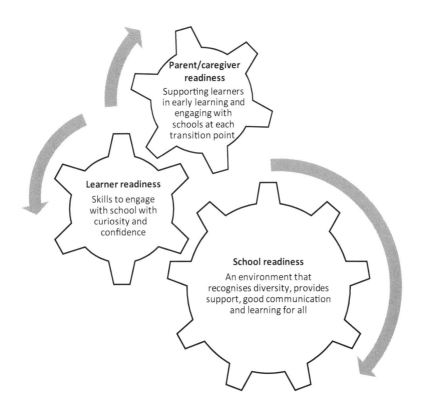

Figure 7.2 The importance of readiness and connectivity to support transition

- *I was aware of doing what might be seen as assessments before going to primary school. I think to see if I was ready or not. We were observed and they were like puzzles. Not all children went to primary school at six* (L, Germany).

Pedagogies of educational transitions and their influences

White (2007) explored how pedagogy can influence transitions and how specific approaches can be built into the curriculum and learning and teaching approaches. He discusses developing confidence and comfort in learners. An example of this can be seen in New Zealand where there are schools that manage the transition from primary to secondary education. They keep elements of the primary environment, for example, a home room where some classes are taught, and learners are only required to move for some specialist classes. This is in line with the work of Ballam et al (2016) about international perspectives on the pedagogies of educational transitions which considers the entering of primary school the most critical transition of all.

In France, the curricula for settings for the first three years of primary education have been developed according to a single framework (setting the common principles that learning must be inclusive, help pupils better understand the world and adopt rational approaches, as well as foster critical thinking and democratic ideals). In Slovenia, the kindergarten and school curricula were developed as part of the same curricular reform (1996–1999) with the principle that education programmes have to be consistent and aligned vertically and horizontally. Similar subject areas (ie languages, art, environment, mathematics) are covered in both frameworks, especially for the first three-year cycle of basic school (offering integrated primary and lower-secondary education). In Finland, the national curricula for Early Childhood Education and Care (ECEC), pre-primary education and primary education are aligned and complement each other with the aim of building a continuous learning path for the child. According to these three curricula, local providers are required to ensure alignment, co-ordination and co-operation in the development of their local level curricula from ECEC to primary education (OECD, 2019b).

The rise of the relevance of play-based curricula can be seen particularly in Scandinavia and the UK as the countries try and develop curious and confident learners to prepare them to deal with transition and change on their learning journey.

Increasingly there are curriculum models that provide flexibility for learners and a movement away from key stages of development. In Wales, the Successful Futures review of the curriculum and assessment procedures (Donaldson, 2015) discusses a continuum of learning and the importance of increasing potential and attainment by minimising transitions and changes. The review advocates a clear line of sight from start to finish of the curriculum journey rather than seeing it as a series of blocks or stages.

Arnold et al (2007) consider the steps from across the globe to provide more continuity by focusing on the importance of an integrated curriculum for the learner journey. The *Step by Step Transition Primary School Programme* (Arnold et al, 2007) makes recommendations that could be considered at all transition points and not just from preschool to primary:

- *trying to keep children within positive friendship groups during transition;*
- *pupils from the school to talk to new pupils about their experiences;*
- *teachers and parents look at the curriculum from the next stage together to help prepare children;*
- *a curriculum that uses the same pedagogic framework, considers the individuals learning needs and progress, learning environment, family participation, teaching strategies for meaningful learning, planning and assessment, professional development and social inclusion.*

Context: environment, policy and culture

There is a clear need to research, develop and implement effective integrated transition policies and practices to ensure that learners start their learning journey well and are scaffolded in an appropriate way throughout their learning journey. When the ideas and approaches of different countries are considered, as well as the context in which they are operating, it is clear that some can be transferred. However, they are dependent on a range of variables being in place. For example, learners in the Scandinavian countries appear to have fewer difficulties in their transitions than many young people in the rest of Europe. There are variations in the transition pathways and current transition policies but it seems that in comparison to most European countries, the Scandinavian countries offer stronger, multi-dimensional social support for all young people, which reduces risks associated with their transitions particularly after leaving compulsory school. Helms Jørgensen et al (2019) undertook a comparative analysis of transition in Sweden, Finland and Denmark. Two key messages from their research are the importance of monitoring the impact of changes in policy making and the need to make young people more individually responsible for the success of their transitions. Despite this, Vallberg-Roth (2014) found that the revised Swedish policy documents for preschool tended to focus mostly on teaching and learning, with well-being, security and care becoming less prominent.

further education

The majority of this chapter has focused on transitions into the compulsory sector and the compulsory sector itself. Greatbatch and Tate (2019) explore transition in and from further education in 12 countries. For example, in Canada, transitional programmes for low attainers are often targeted at young people towards the end of their compulsory education to support the move into post-compulsory education. According to Greatbatch and Tate (2019) the Options and Opportunities programme in Nova Scotia targets high-school students who may be disengaged from school and are not achieving their academic potential, offering them alternative options to traditional learning. The programme aims to provide students with the opportunity to pursue hands-on learning experiences with a career focus and prepare students for successful transitions from high school to a career path. There is a particular emphasis on facilitating transition from lower-level post-secondary programmes (such as one- or two-year programmes) to higher-level programmes (such as three- to four-year bachelor programmes in universities). In Germany, a transition system aims to address competence deficits and prepare young people for further vocational training. Students are also supported to transition back into more academic courses.

International student reflections on their learning journey

The final section of this chapter is based on conversations with international students at a UK university on how their school systems prepared them for their transitions and learner journey. They were asked to reflect on their education experience and how prepared they were to study in a different country. The students from outside the UK talked about independence and being prepared for change.

- *My education experience prepared me to be an independent learner and manage my learning wherever I am* (L2, Germany).
- *Coming to another place to study was not really frightening for me. Although the teaching approaches are different here we were always encouraged to see change and difference as a good thing* (L1, The Netherlands).

Students from Germany talked about the fact that different routes for education were all equally valued and that vocational learning had a high status. This had a positive impact on their transition into work and how they balanced work and academic study.

- *On vocational courses, we are used to studying and working at the same time and this helps us to learn how to be part of an organisation and study at the same time. We are all here with industry experience that we can relate to our course* (L2, Germany).

One student commented that UK students seemed to expect more support for their learning and questioned whether more should be done to make them more independent and resilient learners.

- *There is much more support for the learner here. At home we are expected to take responsibility for our learning from a young age* (L1, South Korea).

Students from the UK who chose to study in another country commented that change and being exposed to different types of learning was an important transition experience that made them look at learning in different ways.

- *Coming out of my comfort zone and going to study abroad in Sweden was the best thing for me. The experience helped me to transition into being a more confident and critical learner* (L1, UK student on Erasmus Exchange to Sweden).

Conclusion

The ET2020 Working Group on Schools in its final report for the European Commission (European Commission, 2018a) examined successful, emerging or potential new policy developments in EU member states and the following were identified as relevant to the study of transitions:

- supporting learners and parents to make informed choices about their education;
- effective inter-institutional collaboration between all sectors to effectively scaffold the learning journey supported by accurate data;
- embedding pedagogical approaches to support transitions.

This chapter has provided some foundations on which to explore approaches and attitudes to transitions from different perspectives. Bronfenbrenner's ecological systems model (1979) provides a useful lens. The macrosystem is the wider context of international research into transitions. There is also some reference to the meso- and microsystems for specific examples of practice. The theme of *readiness for education* from a pupil, parent and school perspective and how this can be supported is critical. The initial experience of the learner has a significant impact on their learning journey and the transitional stages that they face. Discussions with learners who have experienced different school systems provide insights on approaches, levels of scaffolding and their resilience to cope with change as they move through the education system.

The three models in Europe illustrate the diverse approaches to managing curriculum and the stages of the learner journey. It is critical that these approaches are looked at in context and consider the political, social, and educational framework of the countries. The OCED annual *Education at a Glance* reports provide country profiles to support your exploration transitions in different countries.

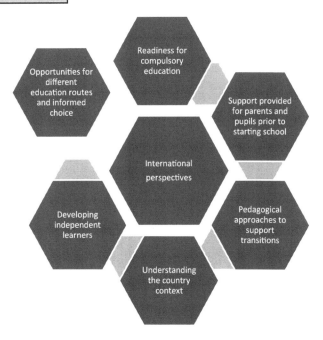

Figure 7.3 Lesson for transition from international perspectives

When considering an approach to managing a transition the following points should be considered.

- The opportunities to decide whether a child is ready for education are approached in very different ways. In many countries age is the only criteria, but is this appropriate?
- There is evidence to show that there are very different levels of educational and financial support available for preschool education and this must be acknowledged when looking at the different systems.
- Some pedagogical approaches are more mindful of transition and the curriculum is designed to support this.
- In order to understand why a country approaches transitions in the way that it does, you must be mindful of the country context. Some approaches may not be transferable to other contexts.
- How much support should we provide for transitions? There are different opinions about the amount of support that is needed.
- How flexible can education systems be to support different learner strengths and needs and acknowledge that transitions may take place at different times and provide different learning paths when needed?

❖ Reflective questions

1. How ready are your learners and their parents for the transition into formal education? Explore cases where deferral would be beneficial.

2. Would starting compulsory education at seven years old work in the UK? Explain your ideas for and against this proposal.

3. How can we prepare our learners to be resilient and self-reliant as they progress through the education system?

4. Which countries would you like to explore in more detail to find out about how they manage key transitions for learners?

5. The importance of collaboration between education settings is critical. How much collaboration are you aware of between settings in your practice?

Suggested reading

Arnold, C, Bartlett, K, Gowani, S and Merali, R (2007) Is Everybody Ready? Readiness, Transition and Continuity – Reflections and Moving Forward. [online] Available at: https://files.eric.ed.gov/fulltext/ED522694.pdf (accessed 27 February 2020).

The point at which a child is ready to enter compulsory education is a critical consideration and this commissioned paper explores readiness and transition through three areas: children and their 'readiness'; schools and their 'readiness'; and the implications for policy and practice. It is a good starting point to explore this area.

Lally, V and Doyle, L (2012) Researching Transitions in Learning and Education: International Perspectives on Complex Challenges and Imaginative Solutions *Research in Comparative and International Education*, 7(4): 394–408. [online] Available at: https://doi.org/10.2304%2Frcie.2012.7.4.394 (accessed 12 August 2020).

This special edition of the journal of *Research in Comparative and International Education* encourages the reader to explore international perspectives on transition and brings together a series of papers to support us to think differently about how we view transitions.

European Commission (2018) Continuity and Transitions in Learner Development: Guiding Principles for Policy Development on Learner Pathways and Transitions in to School Education. [online] Available at: https://ec.europa.eu/education/sites/education/files/document-library-docs/education-training-et2020-working-groups-2016-2017_en.pdf (accessed 12 August 2020).

There are excellent policy documents produced by the European Commission. The content comes from a 'research with member countries' exercise, and a peer-learning activity. It acknowledges the personal nature of the learning journey from early years and through schools to post-compulsory education and the importance of the experiences of the individual learner.

References

Ackesjö, H (2013) Children Crossing Borders: School Visits as Initial Incorporation Rites in Transition to Preschool Class. *International Journal of Early Childhood*, 45: 387–410. [online] Available at: https://doi.org/10.1007/s13158-013-0080-7 (accessed 7 June 2020).

Arnold, C, Bartlett, K, Gowani, S and Merali, R (2007) Is Everybody Ready? Readiness, Transition and Continuity – Reflections and Moving Forward. [online] Available at: https://files.eric.ed.gov/fulltext/ED522694.pdf (accessed 27 February 2020).

Ballam, N, Parry, B and Garpelin, A (2016) *Pedagogies of Educational Transitions* Basel: Springer.

Bronfenbrenner, U (1979) *The Ecology of Human Development: Experiments by Nature and Design*. Boston, MA: Harvard University Press.

Bronfenbrenner, U (1989) Ecological Systems Theory. *Annals of Child Development*, 6: 187–259.

Broström, S (2012) Children's Participation in Research. *International Journal of Early Years Education*, 20: 257–69. [online] Available at: https://doi.org/10.1080/09669760.2012.715407 (accessed 7 June 2020).

Donaldson, G (2015) Successful Futures: Independent Review of Curriculum and Assessment Arrangements in Wales. [online] Available at: https://dera.ioe.ac.uk/22165/2/150225-successful-futures-en_Redacted.pdf (accessed 27 February 2020).

Dunlop, A W (2003) *Bridging Children's Early Education Transitions Through Teacher Collaboration*. Paper presented at the New Zealand Association for Research in Education and Australian Association for Research in Education Joint Conference, November 29–December 3, Auckland, Australia.

Ecclestone, K, Biesta, G and Hughes, M (2010) (eds) *Transitions Through the Lifecourse*. London: Routledge.

European Commission (2018a) European Ideas for Better Learning: The Governance of School Education Systems. Final report and thematic outputs of the ET2020 Working Group Schools. [online] Available at https://ec.europa.eu/education/policies/european-policy-cooperation/et2020-working-groups_en (accessed 27 February 2020).

European Commission (2018b) Continuity and Transitions in Learner Development: Guiding Principles for Policy Development on Learner Pathways and Transitions in to School Education. [online] Available at: https://ec.europa.eu/education/sites/education/files/document-library-docs/education-training-et2020-working-groups-2016-2017_en.pdf (accessed 7 June 2020).

European Commission/EACEA/Eurydice (2018) *The Structure of the European Education Systems 2018/19: Schematic Diagrams*. Eurydice Facts and Figures. Luxembourg: Publications Office of the European Union. [online] Available at: https://eacea.ec.europa.eu/national-policies/eurydice/sites/eurydice/files/the_structure_of_the_european_education_systems_2018_19.pdf (accessed 27 February 2020).

European Commission/EACEA/Eurydice (2019) *Key Data on Early Childhood Education and Care in Europe – 2019 Edition*. Eurydice Report. Luxembourg: Publications Office of the European Union.

[online] Available at: https://eacea.ec.europa.eu/national-policies/eurydice/sites/eurydice/files/kd_ecec_2019_report_en.pdf (accessed 27 February 2020).

Greatbatch, D and Tate, S (2019) *International Comparisons of Post-Compulsory Education Systems*. London: Department for Education.

Helms Jørgensen, C, Järvinen, T and Lundahi, L (2019) A Nordic Transition Regime? Policies for School-to-Work Transitions in Sweden, Denmark and Finland. *European Educational Research Journal*, 18(3): 278–97. [online] Available at: https://doi.org/10.1177%2F1474904119830037 (accessed 7 June 2020).

Lally, V and Doyle, L (2012) Researching Transitions in Learning and Education: International Perspectives on Complex Challenges and Imaginative Solutions. *Research in Comparative and International Education*, 7(4): 394–408. [online] Available at: https://doi.org/10.2304%2Frcie.2012.7.4.394 (accessed 7 June 2020).

Larsen, B, Jensen, L and Jensen, T P (2014) Transitions in Secondary Education: Exploring Effects of Social Problems. *Research in Social Stratification and Mobility*, 38: 32–42. [online] Available at: https://doi.org/10.1016/j.rssm.2014.05.001 (accessed 7 June 2020).

Nielsen, L, Shaw, T, Meilstrup, C B, Koushede, V, Bendtsen, P, Rasmussen, M and Cross, D (2017) School Transition and Mental Health Among Adolescents: A Comparative Study of School Systems in Denmark and Australia. *International Journal of Educational Research*, 83: 65–74. [online] Available at: http://dx.doi.org/10.1016/j.ijer.2017.01.011 (accessed 7 June 2020).

OECD (2019a) *Education at a Glance 2019: OECD Indicators*. Paris: OECD Publishing. [online] Available at: https://doi.org/10.1787/f8d7880d-en (accessed 7 June 2020).

OECD (2019b) *PISA 2018 Results (Volume III): What School Life Means for Students' Lives*. PISA, Paris: OECD Publishing. [online] Available at: https:// doi.org/ 10.1787/ acd78851- en (accessed 7 June 2020).

Rouse, C E, Brooks-Gunn, J and McLanahan, S (2005) Introducing the Issue. *The Future of Children*, 15(1): 5–14. [online] Available at: https://doi.org/10.1353/foc.2005.0010 (accessed 13 June 2020).

Studying in Germany (2020) German Education System. [online] Available at: https://studying-in-germany.org/german-education-system/ (accessed 27 February 2020).

UNESCO (2012) *International Standard Classification of Education ISCED* 2011. Montreal: UNESCO Institute for Statistics. [online] Available at: http://uis.unesco.org/sites/default/files/documents/international-standard-classification-of-education-isced-2011-en.pdf (accessed 27 February 2020).

UNICEF (2012) School Readiness and Transitions. [online] Available at: https://unicef.org/publications/files/CFS_School_Readiness_E_web.pdf (accessed 27 February 2020).

Vallberg-Roth, A-C (2014) Nordic Comparative Analysis of Guidelines for Quality and Content in Early Childhood Education. *Nordic Early Childhood Education Journal*, 8(1): 1–35. [online] Available at: https://doi.org/10.7577/nbf.693 (accessed 7 June 2020).

White, C B (2007) Smoothing Out Transitions: How Pedagogy Influences Medical Students' Achievement of Self-Regulated Learning Goals. *Advances in Health Sciences Education Theory and Practice*, 12(3): 279–97. [online] Available at: https://doi.org/10.1007/s10459-006-9000-z (accessed 7 June 2020).

8. CONCLUSION

In this book, transitions have been looked at from a number of different stakeholders' perspectives and in relation to a range of theories. By combining theories of transition with stakeholders' voices, the authors have endeavoured to provide real-life examples of various transitions, and how stakeholders perceive them. A key aim of this book has been to encourage you to consider recommendations for future transitions and to reflect upon transitions using key questions alongside suggested reading. This concluding chapter considers what has been learnt from the overarching themes and key issues that cross between chapters.

As stated in Chapter 1 this book has taken a fresh perspective on transition moving away from viewing transition as a one-off event that is done *to* children and towards conceptualising transition through issues of identity as well as developmental and emotional changes. Throughout this book, the chapters, which have focused upon the theory of transition linked to real-life practice, are heard through the voice of all the stakeholders involved. Chapter 2 framed transitions thorough a number of theoretical lenses, which have underpinned this book. Key theories have been explored – Bronfenbrenner's (1979) ecological systems theory, Vygotsky's (1978) sociocultural theory of cognitive development, life-course theory developed by Hutchison (2011), communities of practice theory (Lave and Wenger, 1991) and *Les Rites De Passage* (van Gennep, 2019). Throughout the chapter, each theory was discussed including how it has helped to inform an awareness of the role of the learner, the practitioners and other key stakeholders involved in the transition process.

Chapter 3 focused upon transition experiences for vulnerable learners with a range of additional learning needs. Here practitioners were asked to reflect upon your transition processes to ensure that experiences are tailored and appropriate to the individual learner and their needs. This chapter discussed the need for partnership and collaboration between parents, caregivers and the learner themselves to ensure that the transition process is as smooth as possible. This chapter included quotes from a number of stakeholders on the transition process for those with additional or special learning needs. It discussed how settings have facilitated or adapted transition processes to engender a sense of belonging and effective engagement for these vulnerable learners.

Chapter 4 focused on the voice of the learners from those at the very start of their transition into education through to those studying at post-compulsory level. It discussed how learners prepare for transition, the actual transition process and transition outcomes. It explored the different ways settings prepare learners for transition and analysed learners' perceptions of the different transitions they have experienced, both positive and negative. One theme that emerged in this chapter was the experience of learners in mixed-aged classes. There was a feeling that there needed to be a reconceptualization of the transition process with separate transition events for different aged learners. Links were made between the learner experiences and the theories explored in Chapter 2 with a consideration of the importance of the relationship between the learner and the wider learning environment (Bronfenbrenner, 1979) and the more knowledgeable other (Vygotsky, 1978). Additionally, this chapter debated the duration of transition through life-course theory (Hutchison, 2011) as being not a one-off event but an ongoing process.

Chapter 5 considered transition from the perspective of parents and caregivers including evidence that their social and emotional response to their child's transition is often overlooked. There is little evidence of support for parents regarding their own socio-emotional well-being during their children's transitions. This chapter also found that more research needs to be completed around what parents and caregivers can add to the transition process and what support can, in turn, be offered to them. To achieve this there needs to be more consideration of effective communication between settings and parents and caregivers, allowing the transitional process to become more beneficial for all involved. There needs to be a consideration of parents' own experiences and perceptions of education as this can affect how they support their child's transitions. This links to Bronfenbrenner's theory (1979) where the relationship parents and caregivers have with settings and other stakeholders has a significant impact on the learner's academic achievement and general well-being. The parent can be considered the more knowledgeable other in preparing the child for transition, thus linking to Vygotsky's (1978) theory. Through effective ongoing links and communication with settings, parents and caregivers can feel equal partners in the transitional process and this can lead to more effective transitions.

Chapter 6 moved the transition story onto the role of practitioners in the process. This was discussed through effective planning, smooth co-ordination of activities and the meaningful relationships built up with all stakeholders involved in the transition process. Comments from interviews with practitioners in this chapter explored how settings initially prepare learners through familiarising events and *'getting to know you'* activities. Practitioners emphasised the importance of building relationships with the learners and helping to build up their resilience to support ongoing transitions. Settings used a number of different events in preparing children for transition into their new classes. These ranged from *'walkabouts'* and activities to enthuse and stimulate the children to giving them opportunities to experience a new playground such as the *'big yard'*. The role of the practitioner was considered as preparing the *'bridge'* for the children to cross into their new setting. In addition, practitioners need to send and receive information about learners to ensure the transition process is as seamless as possible. Practitioners also felt that the transition process had a wider remit around developing resilience in learners throughout their life journey. This resonates with the communities of practice theory (Lave and Wenger, 1991) whereby practitioners draw upon their own experiences to enhance the competencies of the transition process. Practitioners also often sought feedback from learners and key stakeholders giving them the opportunities to reflect upon their transition processes. This was important to allow the practitioners to change or amend transition processes thus viewing transition as not being static but a fluid process responding to learners' and stakeholders' needs.

Chapter 7 looked at transitions from an international perspective. It considered how different countries carry out transitions. Using Bronfenbrenner's ecological systems approach (1979) as a framework, this chapter explored some of the commonalities and differences of how transitions are approached in a global context. It looked at the different ages children start school in different

European countries and how some countries allow children to defer starting schooling until they are developmentally ready. Differences between the structures of schooling were examined and three main models were considered:

- single-structure education providing compulsory schooling throughout with no transition between primary and secondary education;
- common core curriculum where, once primary education has been completed, all students progress to secondary education;
- differentiated branches where, after completion of primary education, students follow distinct educational pathways and some countries offer vocational, technical or general education tracks.

The chapter included discussions with international learners on their educational experiences of different school systems and the transitions they faced. It considered the strengths and weaknesses of the differing approaches and debated the concept of school readiness. This chapter allowed you the opportunity to reflect upon the different approaches adopted by differing countries and to consider whether the approach adopted by the UK is the most appropriate. This is timely as Wales prepares to move from the common core curriculum model as seen in England to the single-structure approach adopted by Scandinavian countries.

Throughout this book the overarching theme of transition preparations, processes and outcomes has been framed by the theories explored in Chapter 2. Different chapters have presented the voices of the learners, stakeholders and practitioners and their opinions and experiences of transitions. This has encouraged you to develop an understanding of the many themes that shape transition.

The innovative approach to understanding transitions across age ranges, from the perspective of different stakeholders and in different contexts, should help you to develop your own practice. This book is not just about *what* transition is but is also about the *why* of transition and *how* to do it effectively. It is about collaboration and partnership between all stakeholders involved in the transition process. It is about how to get it right from the very start and continuing to get it right, thus benefitting all learners of all ages.

References

Bronfenbrenner, U (1979) *The Ecology of Human Development: Experiments by Nature and Design*. Boston, MA: Harvard University Press.

Hutchison, E D (2011) Life Course Theory. In Levesque R J R (eds) *Encyclopaedia of Adolescence*. Springer, New York, NY.

Lave, J and Wenger, E (1991) *Situated Learning: Legitimate Peripheral Participation*. Cambridge, UK: Cambridge University Press.

van Gennep, A (2019) *The Rites of Passage* (second edition). Chicago: University of Chicago Press.

Vygotsky, L S (1978) *Mind in Society. The Development of Higher Psychological Processes.* Cambridge, MA: Harvard University Press.

Wenger, E (1998) *Communities of Practice: Learning, Meaning, and Identity.* New York: Cambridge University Press.

ALL CHANGE!

INDEX

Bold numbers denote tables

ALL CHANGE!